WEDDING
SPEECHES
FOR WOMEN

If you want to know how...

Be the *Best* Best Man and Make a Stunning Speech
Philip Khan-Panni

'Essential reading, and a great gift for those preparing to
stand and deliver on the big day.' – *Wedding Day*

Make a Great Wedding Speech
Philip Calvert

This book will thoroughly prepare the speechmaker to deliver his or her
speech with an originality which reflects the speaker's personality and a
propriety to match the particular circumstances of the occasion itself.

howtobooks

Send for a free copy of the latest catalogue to:
How To Books
3 Newtec Place, Magdalen Road,
Oxford OX4 1RE, United Kingdom
email: info@howtobooks.co.uk
http://www.howtobooks.co.uk

WEDDING
SPEECHES
FOR WOMEN

Suzan St Maur

howtobooks

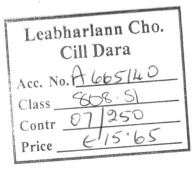
Published by How To Books Ltd,
3 Newtec Place, Magdalen Road,
Oxford OX4 1RE. United Kingdom.
Tel: (01865) 793806. Fax: (01865) 248780.
email: info@howtobooks.co.uk
http://www.howtobooks.co.uk

British Library Cataloguing in Publication Data
A catalogue record for this book is available from the British Library

ISBN-13: 978-1-84528-107-6
ISBN-10: 1-84528-107-1

Cover design by Mousemat Design Limited
Cartoons © Colin Shelbourn, www.shelbourn.com
Produced for How To Books by Deer Park Productions, Tavistock, Devon
Typeset by PDQ Typesetting, Newcastle-under-Lyme, Staffs.
Printed and bound by Bell & Bain Ltd, Glasgow

NOTE: The material contained in this book is set out in good faith for general
guidance and no liability can be accepted for loss or expense incurred as a result of
relying in particular circumstances on statements made in the book. The laws and
regulations are complex and liable to change, and readers should check the current
position with the relevant authorities before making personal arrangements.

Contents

Part 3: Content Resources

Dedication

To 'FallingSideways'

The brilliant rock band created by my son Tom and his friends
Jackson, James and Oli, whose practice sessions serenaded me on
many occasions while I was writing this book. (And don't forget
to try to squeeze in some schoolwork.)

http://www.fallingsideways.org

The author

Canadian-born Suzan St Maur has been a professional writer for more years than she cares to admit to. Although she started out working as a journalist and an advertising copywriter, during the 1990s and into the new millennium she became well-known as one of the UK's leading business speechwriters. She has written words for many of the UK's captains of industry, plus politicians, TV personalities, actors and more.

Having become a familiar name in business speechwriting Suze (as everyone calls her) began getting requests to turn her hand to writing cabaret scripts and social speeches, in addition to the business material. Attacking these projects with gusto, she then gained a reputation as quite a useful comedy/social speechwriter in addition to the accolades she received in the business world.

Apart from the speechwriting Suze runs a successful business writing and coaching consultancy, as well as having written a number of books (on consumer, business and humour topics) of which this is number 13 – not ominous, we hope!

Suze lives in a village near Milton Keynes, central England, with her teenage son Tom and various dogs and cats. For more information on Suze check out her website here: *www.suzanstmaur.com*

Other books by Suzan St Maur
The Jewellery Book (with Norbert Streep) (Magnum)
The Home Safety Book (Jill Norman Books)
The A to Z of Video and AV Jargon (Routledge)

Writing Words That Sell (with John Butman) (Management Books, 2000)

Writing Your Own Scripts and Speeches (McGraw Hill)

The Horse Lover's Joke Book (Kenilworth Press)

Powerwriting: the hidden skills you need to transform your business writing (Prentice Hall Business)

Canine Capers: over 350 jokes to make your tail wag (Kenilworth Press)

The Food Lover's Joke Book (ItsCooking.com)

Get Yourself Published (LeanMarketing Press)

The MAMBA way to make your words sell (LeanMarketing Press)

The Easy Way To Be Brilliant At Business Writing (LeanMarketing Press)

Successful Business Writing In English (with Frances Gordon) (LeanMarketing Press, due 2006)

Acknowledgements

There are so many people I want to thank that I think the only fair way is to list them alphabetically:

Anya
Caroline Lashley
Christine Knott
Dawn Charles
Debbie Jenkins
Elizabeth Lorkins
Evelyn and Phillip Khan-Panni
Gail Cornish
Helen Parkinson
Jo Parfitt
Joan McFarlane
John Bowden
Julie Lacey
Kenilworth Press
Lesley Chapman
Maja Pawinska Sims
Nikki Read and Giles Lewis
Philip Calvert
Sharon Thornton
(Dr) Simon Raybould
Tom Webb

...plus all the staff and patients at the Milton Keynes Macmillan Oncology Unit, whom I bored rigid with stories about 'my book' every three weeks.

Thank you all for your help, contributions and support.

Introduction

Hello and welcome to *Wedding Speeches For Women* – as far as
we know, the first contemporary book on that topic to be
published in the UK.

Although it's quite common at the moment for 'the bride to get
up and say a few words as well', there's a big difference between
that and at least an equal share of the most important speeches
being given by not only the bride, but also the maid or matron
of honour, the bride's or groom's mother, grandmother, aunt,
daughter, god-daughter, best friend or anyone else of a female
persuasion. Yet that's the direction in which society is moving
now.

Of course there are many good books in existence which tell the
men how to make their speeches, and you'll probably find some
useful pointers if you have a look at those too (see Resources,
page 201). But books for the men aren't enough for us women,
for two reasons.

One, the men tend usually to make the same, traditional speeches
in which they must observe conventions and say what's expected
of them. We girls, having been ignored in the days when those
traditions and conventions were established, are now delightfully
free from such restrictions. So we can pretty well say what we
like.

Two, whether the arch-feminists like it or not, there is a
difference in appropriate presentation styles between men and
women. Men might get away with being a little naughty or
smutty in a wedding speech, but coming from a woman it usually

sounds tacky and cheap. We girls need to be cleverer and subtler – which shouldn't be hard, considering our infinitely superior brains!

Anyway, in this book I have shared all my own speechwriting skills (see my author bio for details of those) and I have also enlisted the help of a number of women who have made wedding speeches themselves. You can share their contributions in the pages that follow.

I hope the book will give you all the help you need to make *the* starring speech at your wedding or that of your relative or friend. Please don't hesitate to email me if you have any questions about the book's contents, or anything else that might be concerning you about your speech – *suze@suzanstmaur.com* – and I'll get back to you as soon as I can.

I wish you happy reading and happy speech-making!

Suze

Part 1

It's Easy When You Know How

Planning –
The Foundation of Success

How far you can dictate the planning of your wedding speech depends of course on where you are in the pecking order. If you're the bride, that's great – it's your call! If you're a female relative or friend, however, you may not get the opportunity to do more than make tactful suggestions. It will probably help you a lot to understand how wedding speeches *should* be planned, because if nothing else it means your own speech will benefit.

TRADITIONAL WEDDING SPEECHES

To do a proper job of this we need to go back to the traditional set up of male-only speeches, largely because in the UK at least most weddings still follow that basic structure, i.e.:

- **The father of the bride (or other close male relative of hers, or sometimes an old family friend)**
  He talks about the bride – usually makes her squirm with embarrassment at the anecdotes of the bride aged five with her teddy bears and dolls! He welcomes the guests to the wedding and the groom and his family into his own. He will also thank people for their efforts in the wedding preparations (especially the bride's mother, if appropriate) and mention special guests who can't be present. Finally he proposes a toast to the bride and groom.

- **The bridegroom**
  He normally speaks on behalf of both himself and the bride, thanking the bride's father for his speech, and to all the family members concerned in setting up and paying for the wedding. He also thanks everyone else for their roles on the day and the entire audience for their gifts, etc. He ends by proposing a toast to the bridal attendants (bridesmaids, maid/matron of honour, pages, etc.)

- **The best man**
  He thanks the bridegroom for his speech and – on behalf of the bridal attendants – for his toast. He talks about the groom, and his relationship with him. He then reads out any telemessages and cards that have accumulated, and ends by proposing a toast to the bride and groom.

So, now that we are about to throw that structure into disarray by introducing women speakers into the equation, let's strip out what we need to consider as essentials. These are the elements that need to be incorporated into the wedding speeches no matter who gives them. Obviously each family will have their own particular priorities, but here are the basics as I see them.

WHAT IS THE PURPOSE OF WEDDING SPEECHES?

1. *For the key participants to show appreciation to and thank publicly:*
   - everyone who has worked hard to make the day a success
   - everyone who has contributed financially
   - everyone who has come to the wedding, especially from far away
   - everyone who has sent or brought gifts to the bridal couple
   - everyone who has participated in the ceremony – bridal attendants, minister/priest/rabbi, etc.

2. *To celebrate the bride and groom and their relationship*

As we'll see later in the book, women's speeches can be positioned in one of two ways – either replacing one of the key traditional male roles, or as an addition/alternative to the traditional male roles. And despite potential grumblings from great uncles, as long as the basic courtesies are covered by the speeches at a wedding, it doesn't really matter who says what.

WORKING OUT A PLAN WITH THE OTHER SPEAKERS

One of the few advantages of the traditional, male-led speech structure is that each speaker knows what his remit is and with luck no one gets left off the thank you list. When that structure is deviated from, though, there is an increased risk that a) someone or something will get forgotten and b) speakers may duplicate each other's content.

There is a simple solution to this problem – make a plan. In years gone by sometimes this was geographically difficult, with families and friends not being able to get together to discuss the speech content until perhaps the night before the wedding. However, these days with cheaper telephone charges and the luxury of email, those old excuses for not communicating with your fellow speakers in plenty of time have been eradicated.

The act of creating a plan will ensure that all essential elements of the speeches are catered for and, hopefully, allocated fairly among the speakers. It will also avoid duplication which can be a killer. There's nothing so irritating as listening to the speaker before you 'steal your lines', necessitating a hasty rewrite of your speech on a table napkin ten minutes before your big moment.

Never forget whose wedding it is

Now this may seem obvious, but the best place to start when making the plan is with the bride and groom. Even if you are the bride, you can sometimes be forgiven for wondering whose day this is going to be, especially when mothers are in charge of organisation (that's personal experience talking here!).

However, even if the dinner menu and flower arrangements do become someone else's domain, the speeches are entirely centred on the bridal couple, radiating out to their family and friends who are supporting their day. It makes a lot of sense, therefore, for both bride and groom to work very closely with the other speakers right from the planning stage so that not only everyone knows who is going to say what, but also that what everyone is going to say meets with the bridal couple's approval. Which leads neatly on to...

POLITICAL/SOCIAL 'ISSUES' – i.e. PROBLEMS

With so many families having experienced divorce, remarriage, step-parents, step-children, etc., if you're not careful a wedding can turn into an emotional minefield. Although you need to tread warily in what you say in your speech, to be on the safe side you need to allow for any such cans of worms right from the beginning, at the speech planning stage. And that can even start with the decision-making process of who is going to speak in the first place.

THE VOICE OF EXPERIENCE

My sister, the bride, asked me to give the 'bride's father's' speech, as the best solution to the perennial problem of divorced parents. In short, the bride's mother refused to come if the bride's father gave the speech, and the bride's father was embarrassed and upset by the first solution suggested, that the mother's brother give a speech. In the midst of a family crisis my sister called me in floods of tears to ask me to do it, and of course I agreed.

Anya from London

Obviously I can't stick my nose into other families' business and tell you how you should handle delicate issues, but it's essential that everyone stays focused on the fact that a wedding is purely about celebrating the bride and groom's union and happiness – and that's all.

Weddings are not the right time to settle old scores

No matter how difficult relationships between estranged or divorced relatives might be, I personally feel that it's incredibly selfish of them to drag their disputes into such an occasion and upset the bride, groom, or both – as we saw with Anya's poor sister (see above). I know it can be a tense time but there are ways of padding things out so that those who loathe each other are rendered relatively harmless.

For example, you can nominate someone to keep them apart. This job was assigned to me at my brother-in-law's wedding and I had to sit in the front pew between his father and his mother, for whom this was the first full frontal encounter since they had last snarled at each other in the divorce court 30 years previously. It certainly kept me on the edge of my chair, or pew, rather, but they behaved themselves.

Anyway for the sake of the speeches, and after all that's what we are here to talk about, it makes life a great deal more pleasant if any familial animosity is anticipated very early on and planned for before you even consider what to say – or more to the point here what *not* to say – in your speech.

Other prickly issues: disapproval/jealousy

Whether any of us like it or not, you may get a little bit of disapproval from some of the men *and* women involved in the wedding preparations. These are likely to be the older ones who favour the traditional structure and can usually be chivvied along with some cheerful, tactful chat. But be aware of jealousy, too. As you may already know emotions run high on these family occasions and even something as apparently trivial as the seating plan can cause spectacular tantrums.

You might think, with some justification, that if someone is bitchy or resentful about your making a speech it's their problem. However a lot depends on who that person is; if it's someone who may be very helpful to you in your research for your speech, say, it will be well worth your while smoothing over ruffled feathers and making friends with him or her.

Other prickly issues: jokes and humour

We'll get into this topic in much more detail later on, but it's worth considering it at the planning stage too. As we'll see, even a little humour works especially well in wedding speeches but there's nothing worse than inadvertently joking about something that someone, somewhere in the audience, doesn't think is funny at all. For that reason it's a very good idea for all wedding speakers – not just you – to discuss this point amongst yourselves at the planning stage so that no one writes a potentially painful *faux pas* into their speech.

TIMING: DON'T FORGET THE CALLS OF NATURE

Traditionally the speeches are made somewhere around the second half of a stand-up reception and after the main course of a sit-down wedding meal. In the first case there should be few housekeeping problems, but in the second case remember to allow a short period for comfort breaks. Children and elderly guests particularly will not enjoy the speeches very much if they have eaten and drunk their fill and experience urgent calls of nature which they're obliged to ignore until the orations are over.

The timing and announcement of the speeches will be greatly helped if you have a way of controlling things. Hence...

THE BENEFITS OF A TOASTMASTER

Whether a professional toastmaster is used (some venues will supply one as part of the wedding package) or one of the speakers does the honours, it's very useful not only to have each speaker formally introduced, but also to warn guests that the speeches will be starting in X minutes. This gives them their cue for the loo if they need one.

Trained toastmasters know how to raise their voices so they can be heard over the hub-bub. But if you are in a position to choose someone amongst a selection of amateurs, anyone with a loud voice is fine. Traditionally your choice might veer towards a man but some women's voices are able to break glass – any female school teacher or horse riding instructor, for example, will do perfectly. A drama teacher friend of mine who is also a horse show organiser can be heard in the next county across a seven-ring showground, tannoy announcements, vehicle movements, etc., with the odd rumble of thunder thrown in. And all that without a microphone; merely the result of teaching a class of 30 unruly Year 10 performing arts pupils.

Speeches and toasts – who does what

Something else that should be worked in early on is to whom the toasts will be made, and by whom. Toasts can either be made at the end of a speech, or they can be little stand-alone speechettes by themselves, given by another speaker or the toastmaster.

Harking back to the traditional structure again, we see that, at the end of his speech, the father of the bride proposes a toast to the bride and groom; the groom responds and at the end of his speech, toasts the bridal attendants; and finally the best man responds to that and can then propose a final toast if he wants to.

However, the bottom line is that provided the bride and groom and attendants get toasted, you and your fellow speakers can toast whoever else you like. Who toasts whom should be decided at the planning stage, though. That way all 'toasting' speakers have the chance to prepare the short preamble you need to deliver before asking people to do the toast itself – the basic message of which is 'please be upstanding and raise your glasses … ladies and gentlemen, [the bride and groom, mother of the bride, Peter and Wendy, etc.].

More than one language

Many weddings involve a blend of more than one culture and/or language; this can range from a contingent of friends from a foreign country attending the wedding, to the bride or groom (and most of her/his family) being from elsewhere. Depending on how pivotal your speech is within the structure, it may be that you'll think of giving a part of your speech in the other language concerned.

Even if you don't speak that other language yourself, it should be possible for you to learn a couple of sentences. If you say these during your speech it's bound to be well appreciated. Just watch out for any clowns who tell you to say something that turns out to be rude! When in doubt, get it translated back into English first.

ANOTHER WORD ABOUT TIMINGS

How long is a piece of string? That's the riddle-like question we need to ask ourselves when determining how long everyone's wedding speeches should run. When you ask anyone else how long a wedding speech should be, the answer ranges from 'as short as possible' to 'as long as the audience continue to enjoy themselves'.

Someone famous (I forget who...ah, another senior moment) once said in a very un-PC sexist way, 'a speech should be like a woman's skirt; short enough to be interesting, but long enough to cover the subject matter'.

Realistically, short, sharp wedding speeches are more enjoyable for everyone than the long, drawn-out variety. My own feeling is that shorter is better; express what you want to express and finish, unless you're someone who can keep a friendly audience entertained for longer. Good luck at making that judgement!

NOW, THE NEXT STAGE ... THE CHICKEN OR THE EGG?

When I was planning this book I thought long and hard about what to discuss next – the 'what to say', or the 'how to say it'. Much as 'what to say' might logically be placed first, I've always found when helping speakers put presentations together that it's better to work on the mechanics of speech preparation and delivery first.

That way once you get to the 'what to say' you're already feeling comfortable and confident about putting your material together, and because you've worked through some presentation techniques and exercises you know what you'll be able to say effectively – and what you won't. That makes your choice of what to say much easier.

I hope you agree with my reasoning!

Preparation – The More You Do, the Better You'll Be

I know you're busy – particularly if you're the bride – but believe me, it really is worth putting some time aside to prepare your speech properly. First of all, proper preparation will mean your speech probably will be much better than the 'off-the-cuff' variety. And secondly, the fact of having prepared and rehearsed it properly will give you plenty of confidence when you get up there to deliver it.

So, where to start? Well, you may want to start straight in with making notes and bullet points to form a structure, then filling in the details as you go along. For the sake of this book, though, I'm assuming that at this stage you're not yet sure what you want to talk about. In this case the best way to start is to do some research.

RESEARCH: WHO TO TALK TO

If you're the bride, there shouldn't be too many problems here as you're likely to know – or at least know of – all the key people on both sides of the family. But depending on what you decide to talk about in your speech (see Chapter 7) you may want to step beyond the obvious. For example, you might want to find out some of your husband-to-be's deep, dark secrets of the past from people such as his former school teachers, college lecturers, work colleagues, etc., and then surprise him with what you discover!

If you're not the bride you may well want to communicate with other members of the wedding party to get background information for your speech. Working closely with the bride and groom (you don't have to reveal your actual findings to them if you want them to be a surprise on the day) should enable you to get access to whoever you need to speak to. With modern IT and communications it shouldn't be difficult to get in touch even if the people you want to talk to live many miles away.

The next stage is to create appropriate questions that will ensure you get the fullest and most informative answers.

RESEARCH: HOW TO GET GOOD ANSWERS

Formal though it sounds, the best way to get good answers from people for your speech research is to use a structured interviewing format. It doesn't need to sound formal, but by following a structure you'll be sure to get as much information as possible. And, the structure will help both you and the person you're interviewing to cover as much ground as possible.

Rather than reinvent wheels I have included here an excerpt from one of my earlier books, *Powerwriting* (Prentice Hall Books, 2002). This was based on my own interviewing experience for video, audio and printed corporate interviewing over umpty-dump years, and trust me – it works.

Here, then, are some ideas on getting through to someone you've never met before.

INTERVIEWING SOMEONE YOU DON'T KNOW: BREAKING THE ICE

...you can...get to the truth by gaining people's confidence, and that you do by becoming their friend. **How do you befriend your interviewees? You get them to talk about themselves.** And not just their corporate or company selves, either, but their personal selves. Pick up on some small thing to get the conversation going...a golf trophy on a shelf, a picture of some children or pets, an attractive piece of jewellery, the quality of the coffee, the weather. Sometimes you'll find that their demeanour changes abruptly – they soften, smile, relax. Once you've got them going on that, ask their opinion on a small point that's relevant to your project. Then gradually guide the conversation into everything else you want to know.

There are very, very, few people in the industrialised world who positively will not warm to someone whom they believe is genuinely interested in them, their life, and their opinions. Over the years I've conducted literally thousands of corporate interviews, many of which were recorded on video or audio, and in all that time I only failed to get through to two people. One was a seven-foot car factory worker with tattoos everywhere, a small chain through one nostril, and a severe speech impediment. The other was a rock band's road manager who was about to get fried by electric shocks in pouring rain on an open-air stage surrounded by live cables. Everybody else, though, eventually opened up and spoke their thoughts freely.

It's not because I've got a friendly face, large cleavage, bulging wallet or anything else. It's because I genuinely like people and I am genuinely interested in them. Interviewees aren't idiots. **If you're only pretending to be interested in them, they'll know. So you have to *be* interested. Really.** And if you are, you'll get the results you want.

Excerpted from *Powerwriting: the hidden skills you need to transform your business writing* by Suzan St Maur

And whether you know the person or not, here is a list of tips which will help you get the best from the interview itself.

- Base your questions on the news reporters' list of 'who, what, where, when, how and why'. In other words, start each question with one of those words, or something similar.

- Never ask a question that can be answered with a 'yes' or a 'no'. Use the news reporters' list as a basis.
  - *Wrong way*: 'Do you remember what John liked to eat when he was a little boy?'
  - *Right way*: 'In your recollection, what was John's favourite food when he was a little boy?'

- Be tactful and polite – never aggressive.
  - *Wrong way*: 'Surely you remember what John's favourite foods were when he was a little boy?'
  - *Right way*: 'I know it was a long time ago, but what can you remember about John's favourite foods when he was a little boy?'

- If you think the person needs prompting, you can try adding a small suggestion to your question. Be careful not to overdo it or you could put the person off.
  - *Wrong way:* 'In your recollection, what was John's favourite food when he was a little boy? Did he like sausages, chips, ice cream, or what?'
  - *Right way:* 'In your recollection, what was John's favourite food when he was a little boy? Did he like all the usual childhood things, or was there anything special?''

- Always make your questions open-ended, so they invite an answer.
  - *Wrong way:* 'Would you say John liked all the usual childhood foods when he was a little boy?'
  - *Right way:* 'How do you think John's food preferences compared with those of other kids when he was a little boy?'

- Ask for opinions. People love to give their opinions, and these often reveal many interesting points.

- When asking a question, just ask one – don't include more than one key thought, or you will confuse the person you're interviewing.

- When you've asked a question, shut up. Let the person speak. Don't interrupt or attempt to steer what they're saying. If you feel they need encouragement, smile and nod, and/or interject the odd 'really?', 'wow, amazing!', 'you're kidding', etc., to spur them on.

- If they falter or hesitate on an important point, don't press them on it. Ask them something else, then return to your original point later on, remembering to ask the question in a different way so they don't realise it's the same point. You'll be surprised how well that can work.

If you're 'interviewing' people by email, you can still use the
points above in the way you structure your written questions to
people. A tip here: I've always found that people respond much
more fully and enthusiastically to email requests for information if
I provide them with a short 'questionnaire'. Should you merely
ask them to tell you what they can about John when he was a
little boy, usually you'll find the answers that come back are rather
sparse. However, even just a few imaginative questions will trigger
their memories and your information feedback will be far more
meaty.

ASSEMBLING YOUR CONTENT

Hopefully by now you will have lots of ideas of what you want to
talk about in your speech – and we'll go into more about that in
Part 2. For now, though, we're still looking at the nuts and bolts
of how to get your material together. And the next stage to
consider is getting something down on screen or paper; not a
structure or running order yet, merely some ideas – a written
brainstorm, if you like.

If you're good with computers and IT you'll find there are
numerous software programs you can use to create an on-screen
brainstorm. (To find a few, just key 'mind mapping' into the
Google search box. At the time of writing there were a mere
1,170,000 entries under that heading.)

If you're a Luddite like me, you may prefer to use a large piece of
paper and a pen or pencil to scribble down all the elements you'd
like to include in your speech. Don't worry if you think there are
too many; you can reduce them later. Just let yourself go and
express your thoughts freely.

Within all these scribblings, you need to include the 'have to' elements of your speech. What these are depends on your role in the proceedings, but especially if you are replacing one of the key traditional male roles, you will need to be mindful of the obligations discussed in Chapter 1. Also, no matter what your role, you should have worked out with the other speakers what (if any) obligation elements of the day are being allocated to you. Ensure they feature prominently in your scribblings.

Assuming you have started preparations for your speech in plenty of time (and you will, won't you!) after a while you will have amassed a good collection of bullet points. At this point you should compare notes with the bride and groom (if you're not the bride) and with the other speakers, to double check that what you talk about will dovetail neatly in with what the others say on the day.

Once you're satisfied that you're on the right track with your scribbles, the next job is to reduce and order them into a realistic skeleton structure that will form the basis of your speech.

Let's assume you are the bride and you want to speak immediately after your father does, and then hand over to your new husband. First of all, here are some of the scribbles from your brainstorm:

Mum worrying about flowers
  Nancy's dress too tight
    <u>**Welcome/thanks**</u>
      Pete and Brian – school practical joke
        <u>**Dad's speech – thanks**</u>
          Pete and Lilia – from SA

Brian's old girlfriend on plane too
  Brian speaks next? Wants last word?
    Dad – bound to tell story about me losing the hamster
      Dad – tell story about barbecue (hee hee hee)
        <u>**Toast to Brian/Mum/Dad/family**</u>
          Thanks for coming
          <u>**Thanks to Mum/Dad for wedding**</u>

You've underlined the 'obligation' elements, which is good. Now all you have to do is put everything into a logical order, and drop any ideas which are irrelevant or repetitive, which will make your speech too long, or which could upset someone and land you in hot water! Here's what your skeleton structure might look like:

◆ Welcome everyone and thank them for coming.
◆ Thank Dad for compliments and embarrassing stories.
◆ Tell embarrassing story about him (barbecue catching fire).
◆ Thank Mum and Dad for wedding.
◆ Mention Pete and Lilia travelling over from South Africa.
◆ Tell story about Pete and Brian, practical joke at school in Joburg.
◆ Make joke about Brian always wanting last word – typical husband.
◆ 'But first', propose toast to Brian and our families.

Okay. That's a good basis. Now you could start straight in and try to write a script for yourself, but although it may seem superfluous you'll find it very helpful to create an interim stage.

Make notes in small chunks
Here, don't try to write your actual words for the speech. Just add some flesh to those bones. For example:

- **Welcome everyone and thank them for coming** ... am really touched to share this day with my family and good friends ... been really generous with gifts, thanks so much ... really hope you're having a great time ...

- **Thank Dad for compliments and embarrassing stories** ... said I was beautiful, probably needs his glasses changing ... great Dad, love him so much ... knew he would tell that story about the hamster ... will never live it down ...

- **Tell embarrassing story about him (barbecue catching fire)** ... Dad always knows best ... barbecue for their Silver Wedding ... wouldn't let Mum and me help ... whole lot caught fire ... steaks ruined, had to eat salad and dessert ... then bought a book and taught all of us how to do it properly ...

- **Thank Mum and Dad for wedding** ... best parents in the world whether good at BBQs or not ... thanks so much for beautiful wedding ... the best day of my life and Brian's.

- **Mention Pete and Lilia travelling over from South Africa** ... fantastic they could come here all that way ... Pete Brian's best friend when they were at school in Joburg ... wonderful that he and his wife Lilia are here to share our wedding day ... sad we couldn't get out there for their wedding ...

- **Tell story about Pete and Brian, practical joke at school in Joburg** ... Pete and Brian don't know I know about this ... certain maths teacher of theirs called Mrs Entwistle is still around ... very interesting email from her about those two locking the headteacher in his study 'by accident,' oh, yeah? ...

- **Make joke about Brian always wanting last word – typical husband** ... being perfect wife will let him ...

- **'But first', propose toast to Brian and our families** ... all of you, our families and my wonderful husband ... and thanks again for everything.

There. That wasn't hard, was it? And believe it or not, you have already started writing your speech. The key to it is, you're writing naturally.

What you want to say, not what you 'should'

If you keep yourself focused on what you want to say, what emerges will be a natural, genuine-sounding speech that reflects your personality and feelings. If on the other hand you focus on what you feel you 'should' say and the way you feel you 'should' say it, you run the risk of creating a great speech that sounds like it was devised for someone else.

I've lost count of the number of speeches I've listened to (not written by me I hasten to add) that came over as completely different from the personality of the speaker. This happens because:

- Many people believe that giving speeches is a serious art form where the grander the verbiage and more ostentatious and self-important the oratory the more points they'll score with their audience.

- People don't understand the difference between writing for the printed word and writing for the spoken word – so their speech sounds like they're reading it from a book.

Either way, it's wrong, wrong, wrong. If you write stuff for yourself to say that reads like it was written for some pontificating old goat or worse still, for some formal wedding ceremony from the 19th century, you will come across as very two-dimensional, shallow, dishonest and utterly unreal. You will also make yourself very uncomfortable and stumble over the words and phrases, which adds 'incompetent' to the list of goofs in my previous sentence.

Okay, you shouldn't give your wedding speech in the same ribald style you might use to tell a joke to your friends in the changing rooms at the gym or on a girls' night out on the town. But you must *always* be, and write for, yourself and your own personality.

Unless you're a trained actor, the only way you're going to come over well is if you are as at ease as possible with your material. This won't happen if you write words and phrases that may look very eloquent on paper, but which are lumpy mouthfuls to say.

The right style is always conversational. The best speakers always talk to audiences as if they were talking to a friend over a cup of coffee – a natural, friendly, personal style. And how do you achieve that conversational style? Get into a conversation.

Talk and record around those chunks

Some people would take the fleshed out structure we created above and write their speech as an extension of that. If you feel happy and confident doing it that way, great – go ahead. If you don't, though, here's a trick which will help you enormously.

Get an audio recording device. At this point it doesn't matter how old it is – even an ancient cassette tape recorder will do – as long as it works. Sit down in a quiet place, preferably when no one else is around, and talk through each of those fleshed-out points in your speech structure.

Don't imagine that you're doing it to the audience at the wedding. Imagine you're giving the speech over a cup of coffee to that friend I mentioned just now. Relax. Focus on how you feel about each point ... how thrilled you are to see so many old friends and loved ones ... how touched you were by what your Dad said ... how funny the flaming barbecue story was ... and so on.

Let the tape/disc/whatever other technology roll until you've covered every point.

Transcribe and edit

Then (and this is a really boring, but worthwhile job) – transcribe what you have said. If you have a friendly secretary/PA or someone else who is one of those brilliant people who can key in transcripts without going doolally, ask him or her to help you out and then buy a lovely lunch to say thanks! It really will be worthwhile.

Why? Because that transcript will form the basis of your speech in a way that is entirely you without any embellishment that you might impose from elsewhere, or any other external influence that could dilute *your* personality. And with wedding speeches more than any other, that is very important.

So. Once you have the transcript, all you need to do is tidy it up. And here are some tidying aids you might find useful.

Show, don't tell

People use this phrase rather flippantly in order to get people to use more lively adjectives, adverbs and other (preferably) vivid words, but we shouldn't lose sight of its value for a wedding speech.

There's no great mystique to it. Simply look at your transcript (or detailed structure if you haven't followed my advice – OK, I forgive you!) and look at the way you express your feelings. Can you think of more powerful words? Think active, not passive. Think vividly descriptive, not passively descriptive. Use the Thesaurus references I've included in the back of this book, or your own (mind you, *Roget* is pretty good – see Resources, page 202) to find words that really do express your feelings.

Later on we'll see why writing a full script is a useful thing to do, although strictly speaking it is not crucial.

In the meantime here are some of the tips on writing for spoken speech I give to my clients – you may find them useful.

BASIC SPOKEN SPEECHWRITING TIPS

♦ To get a true idea of your own natural speech style, tape record yourself as if you were talking to a friend about the whole subject, then transcribe it.

♦ Write in the style of the transcribed text (or that feels comfortable for you to say) – not how some people think 'public speaking' should be phrased.

- Even if you want to make a formal impression on the audience, avoid long words and clumsy phrases – especially unfamiliar ones you could trip over when your stage nerves are making you edgy.

- Don't use language you wouldn't say in 'real life,' and especially not as crutches to prop up weak content.

- Always write shorter sentences than you do for text, vary the length of them, and never follow one long sentence with another long one.

- When in doubt, read it aloud – if there's anything awkward you'll feel yourself tripping over it.

How to use links

Although your speech should be conversational in tone, the reality is it's a monologue. (You don't really want responses from your audience anyway, because that would be hard to control.) In a dialogue with someone else you'll find that the conversation changes topic naturally through the exchange of ideas and comments. But in a speech you need links to smooth over the joins.

Experienced speakers often will use a change of body stance coupled with a few seconds of silence to signal a change of topic. If you feel comfortable doing that then go ahead, but be careful to carry it out over at least two or preferably three to four seconds, so your audience understands. One of the most important things to remember about delivering your speech is to do it at a far slower speed than you would talk to a friend over a coffee. And that message goes for anything you do in your speech, as well as what you say. The main reason is that people – especially at a wedding where they might have had a few drinks – take longer to absorb information from a speaker some distance away than they would if you were standing close by talking directly to them.

You might be safer, however, to write yourself some verbal links. These can be very simple and informal. They should always be preceded by a short pause, which signals that you've come to the end of a topic. You can then link to the next one with something like:

- Of course, that was all a long time ago. Right now I'd like to get back to why we're here today ...
- Now .. some of you may remember ...
- Before we go any further, I want to tell you about ...

Openers and closers

Many people will tell you that a powerful opening and close of a speech are terribly important and in fact as long as those are good you can say pretty well what you like in between. I don't necessarily agree.

I've seen (and written for) many speakers who have agonised during several sleepless nights over how to start their speech with a big bang at the company sales conference, when all the time a simple, sometimes gently humorous opening is far easier – and more effective. And when it comes to a wedding speech, this is even more relevant.

It helps here if we re-examine just why openers and closers are important in the first place. To put it politely, they help to locate the audience, to act as a signal that you're about to start talking to them or that you've just finished talking to them.

To put it crudely, sometimes the opener at least has to act as an alarm clock – waking the audience up after a narcolepsy-inducing previous speaker – or as a fog horn, warning the audience to settle down, shut up and pay attention.

But even if the speaker prior to you has been intensely boring and has had the whole audience shifting from one numb seatbone to the other for 45 minutes, you don't necessarily have to go out there in a top hat and false nose riding a unicycle to get people's attention. What will get the audience's attention is for you to go out there and be yourself.

Say something amusing, heart-warming, witty, whatever, as long as it's something you would say in 'real life'.

Even if you haven't given a speech before, don't be tempted to open with words like 'I'm not very good at giving speeches but ...'. I can't remember which famous person said 'never explain and never apologise' but in this instance, anyway, they had a point. A wedding speech is not the opening night of a West End or Broadway blockbuster; it's you getting up to say a few words about people you care about. The fact that you don't sound like a polished performer is good, not bad.

However you can start by telling a story, a joke (see Chapters 3 and 11), a poem (see Chapters 4 and 12), or even a relevant quote by a famous person (see Chapter 13). This will instantly signal a major change and have the audience looking forward to what you have to say.

The opener and closer don't have to be earth-shattering, but they do have to be part of you and your material. If you're naturally a quiet, private sort of person there's no way you should struggle with a passionate, emotive ending to your speech, even if others think you should be able to carry it off.

Remember, if you don't think something in your speech will work on the day, you're probably right. A story, joke, anecdote or any other part of the speech you find difficult to deal with when you're writing and practising your speech, will be *very* difficult to deal with when you deliver the speech. Always err on the side of caution; on the day, you'll be glad you did.

A COUPLE OF OTHER WRITING TIPS

Many experienced speech-givers use the 'power of three' as a device to get points across. There's something nice and balanced about the three parts, but it tends to place a lot of emphasis on what you're saying. So save this device for a particularly important bit – for example, your toast:

◆ Please raise your glasses now to the people who put me on this planet ... who raised me to be the person I am now ... and who've made our dreams of a perfect wedding come true today ... my parents, Ron and Kathleen!

◆ Please share this toast with me now to the little girl who loved my bedtime stories ... to the beautiful, talented woman she has become ... and to her happiness in a wonderful marriage with Sanjay ... ladies and gentleman, the bride, Jasmin!

Along similar lines – in fact almost interchangeable lines, really – is the trick of 'repetition.' In much the same way, too, it's a very useful way of stressing an important point.

◆ People might say that marriage is an old-fashioned institution. People might say it's unnecessary. People might say it's not 'cool'. But as we can all see, Patrick and Nicole's wedding today is a shining example of how marriage really is a beautiful thing we all treasure.

◆ I've always believed that loving someone is the purest emotion. I've always believed that loving someone can make you happier than almost anything else in the world. I've always believed that when you find the right partner, there's nothing true love can't beat. And here, today, with Katerina and Elias having tied the knot ... well, my beliefs about love have been proven a hundred times over.

There are other tricks and gismos you can use, of course, but mostly those are intended for the professional speech-maker. And you don't want even to try to emulate a professional speaker unless you happen to be one in the first place. In your wedding speech you need to be *you*.

WHY WRITE A FULL SCRIPT?
Many people feel it isn't necessary to write a full script and, if anything, it's better to work from a few bullet points and appear unrehearsed or spontaneous. My day job as a speech-writer might make me biased, but there are some good reasons why writing a full script can be very helpful.

- It provides a detailed framework if you're an inexperienced speaker.

- It allows you to develop and balance your content more easily.

- It means you don't have to make anything up as you go along.

- It acts as a safety net if you do speak from memory then forget something.

- It keeps you to your allotted time (most speakers present at an average of 120 words per minute, so divide the total word count of your written speech by 120 to get its rough presentation length in minutes).

And in any case, if you don't want to be seen to read from your script, once you've rehearsed it thoroughly you can then develop a few bullet points from it to use on the day.

PREPARING CUE CARDS

This may seem ridiculously obvious and you're probably thinking 'why on earth is she bringing that up? It's hardly rocket science'.

Well of course you're right. But – especially in the flurry of other things you might have to think about in the run-up to the wedding – cue cards prepared in the wrong way can become a real pain.

Why?

1. **They contain the wrong information.** You need to develop the points on the cue cards that remind you of *key elements of your speech* – not just the more obvious points like 'thank Mum and Dad', 'mention Great Aunt Miranda coming all the way from

Warsaw', 'propose a toast to the best man', etc. The way to develop cue cards that will be really helpful is to practise your speech from the full script (see above) and then write up bullet points that signal changes of topic, key points from anecdotes, and above all anything you feel you might forget on the day.

2. **If you drop them they fall down and you may be stuck trying to reorder them in a panic.** There are two ways to get around this problem. One is to number the cards so you can reassemble them easily. The next is not only to number them, but also tie them together so if they fall down they fall as one entity and you simply pick them up again. The way to achieve that is to punch a hole in the corner of each card, then tie something strong through them all with a good, tough knot.

3. **You mislay them.** No matter how careful you are to ensure the cue cards are in your pocket or handbag, accidents happen. When you generate your cue cards, make two or even three copies. Put one in your handbag or pocket, one in your car/briefcase/coat, and give one to a trusted friend. That way you're pretty much covered whatever happens.

Now, before we get into delivery of your speech we need to look at two other important areas of creating it: humour, and (OK, to a lesser extent) how to write a poem for the occasion. Enjoy!

Humour – How to Make It Work Well for You

Many wedding speeches have been ruined by jokes that didn't work, for one reason or another. That's why humour is something to be approached with caution, although used wisely it works superbly well.

If you're not a naturally 'funny' person you won't suddenly transform yourself into one just because you're standing up in front of a group of people. If anything, that tends to make you less, not more funny. So whatever happens don't be persuaded to tell a few jokes if that's something you would never dream of doing informally at a social gathering.

However, there are many ways in which you can use humour
effectively even if you are not Jo Brand, Joan Rivers, or Victoria
Wood –so fear not.

WOMEN CAN BE FUNNY WITHOUT BEING UNFEMININE

I don't want you to think of me as a tedious old trout. But I have
to say I can understand how some people, especially older ones,
might be offended to hear a beautiful blushing bride tell bawdy,
blue jokes in her wedding speech. That's probably the domain of
the best man if there is one – not because it's a masculine
privilege, but because it's boring to all but his few drunken rugby
friends at the back of the room.

However, as you can imagine there is a vast difference between
that and being amusing. In some ways I think women speech
makers have an easier job of making audiences laugh, because
they can get a laugh on a much more subtle level than men can –
especially from the other women in the audience. We girls do not
need four-letter words or side-slapping hysterics; just a smile and
a few choice words.

Anyway you look at it humour, correctly used by women or men,
is one of the most powerful communication tools we have at our
disposal. Incorrectly used, as I intimated above, it can be a recipe
for disaster. But how you use humour for a wedding speech
depends simply – like it does in pretty well all other circumstances
– on using your common sense. That's how you can get everyone
laughing with you, not at you, and avoid hurting anyone's feelings.

So what techniques can we use to harness humour effectively?

UNDERSTAND YOUR AUDIENCE

That's something we speech-writers promote very hard in the context of all types of speeches – political, business, motivational, educational, etc. And the more intimate your audience is, the more important it is to understand them very well if you're going to make a connection with them, never mind make them laugh.

I've already talked about the research you need to do in earlier chapters, and why, so I won't go on about it here. However I will remind you about the point I made that you must uncover any political/familial banana skins beforehand so you avoid slipping on them in your speech. And the easiest way in which you could make that mistake is in using (the wrong kind of) humour.

If your audience and the rest of the bridal party all have a keen sense of humour you won't need to be quite so careful. Sadly, circumstances like this are rare. Let's see, then, how we can minimise the risks while making everyone smile.

First of all, use humour about situations, not people

The butt of many jokes and other humour is a person or group of people, so it's hardly surprising that offence is caused. The more extreme types are obvious – mother-in-law jokes, blonde jokes, women jokes, men jokes – but there are many more subtle ones too.

Then there are the nationality gags. I remember in one year hearing exactly the same joke (in three different languages) told by an American about the Polish, by a Canadian about Newfoundlanders, by a French person about Belgians, by a French-speaking Belgian about the Flemish, and by a Flemish person about the Dutch. But I digress.

Most humour is going to involve people in one way or another. However, as long as the butt of the joke is a situation or set of circumstances, not the people, you're far less likely to upset anyone. And there is an added advantage here.

People will usually identify with a situation

Take this one for example:

> Some people are driving along at night and are stopped by a police car. The officer goes to the driver and warns him that one of the rear lights on his vehicle isn't working. The driver jumps out and looks terribly upset. The officer reassures him that he won't get a ticket, it's just a warning, so there's no problem. 'Oh yes, there is a problem,' says the man as he rushes towards the back of the car. 'If you could see my rear lights it means I've lost my trailer.'

As the butt of the joke is the broken rear light and the loss of the trailer, not the policeman or the driver, no one can be offended. And most people can identify with how that would feel.

A PLAY ON THE WORDS: NOT ALWAYS A WISE CHOICE

Another key issue with humour is wordplays, puns, and anything else that's based on figurative speech, slang, or jargon. The short answer is they don't always work – especially if you have other-language speakers at the wedding. However if the play or *double entendre* is in the concept rather than the words, it probably will work.

These may be funny to us, but would not be understood by anyone who is not a good English speaker (or who is older or otherwise less likely to be up to speed about current affairs, etc.) because there is a play on the words:

♦ Déjà moo: The feeling that you've heard this bull before.

♦ The two most common elements in the universe are hydrogen and stupidity.

These, however, probably would be understood because the humour is in the concept, not in the words themselves:

♦ You don't stop laughing because you grow old. You grow old because you stop laughing.

♦ The trouble with doing something right the first time is that nobody appreciates how difficult it was.

SELF-DEPRECATING HUMOUR

Many cultures – especially British – appreciate speech-makers who use humour against themselves. That's safe, at least, because you don't risk hurting anyone else's feelings, and it can be very funny.

Let's look at two different ways to tell this story during a speech by you, the bride, thanking your father for his opening address. Your father has been bald since he was in his twenties, by the way.

1. I remember when I was little I asked Mum why Dad had so few hairs on his head. She said, 'Because your Dad thinks a lot. You know what they say grass doesn't grow on a busy road.' 'Oh,' I said, 'why have *you* got so *much* hair then, Mum?'

2. I remember when I was little I asked Mum why Dad had so few hairs on his head. She said, 'Because your Dad thinks a lot. You know what they say grass doesn't grow on a busy road.' 'Oh,' I said, 'why have *I* got so *much* hair then, Mum?'

The gag is essentially the same in both versions, only in the second you have turned it against yourself – not your Mum. A safer alternative, unless Mum can take a joke.

Self-deprecating humour is very effective provided that it does not start to verge on the paranoid. Depending on who you are in the speech line-up, a couple of gags against yourself, especially at the beginning of your speech, will possibly help to lighten everything up and get the audience chuckling. However you do not want it to turn into a catalogue of misfortunes. This is a wedding – so stay positive!

JOKES – HOW TO PERSONALISE THEM

Over the years I have collected a database of thousands of jokes which I use to 'switch' for clients' speeches, presentations, cabarets and business theatre. The technique works for any kind of speech, though. Basically what you do is take the hub or kernel of a joke and build up the surrounding story in line with your subject matter. For example:

Original

The food in this hotel is disgusting. What could I do about it? You'd better bring it up at the New Guests' Welcome Meeting.

Adaptation

(As chief bridesmaid) Some of you here will remember that
Cassie's hen night was quite an occasion, in fact my memories of
it aren't all that clear after about the seventh glass of champagne,
but still! One thing I do remember though was that breakfast the
next morning was awful – greasy, cold scrambled eggs and
undercooked kippers. I remember poor Cassie complaining about
it and I told her not to worry, we would bring it up as soon as I
could find the manager.

Original

One day my housework-challenged husband decided to wash his
sweatshirt. Seconds after he stepped into the laundry room, he
shouted to me, 'What setting do I use on the washing machine?'

'It depends,' I replied. 'What does it say on your shirt?'

He yelled back, 'University of Oklahoma.'

Adaptation

(As mother of the bridegroom) I don't want to worry you today of
all days, Sheila, but I think I should warn you that Brian's idea of
being domestic isn't quite what ours is. I remember not that long
ago when he was at our house he decided to wash his favourite
shirt so he took it into the kitchen and put it in the machine.
Then he shouted to me, 'What programme should I put it on,
Mum?''Well it depends,' I said. 'What does it say on your shirt?'

There was a pause for a couple of seconds and then he shouted
back, 'Grantham United F.C.'

Using external sources of jokes and funny lines and then personalising them has the great advantage of offering you a huge choice of material (more of that and where to find it in the resources section at the back of this book). In the meantime though, what about internal humour?

'IN-JOKES' – THE PROS AND CONS

'In-jokes' are jokes which are hilariously funny to a group of people who know each other very well, but are unlikely to raise more than a smile – if that – from an outsider. Correctly used, in-jokes are extremely effective.

They work particularly well for company events where the speaker can send up the boss's golf handicap or the finance director's bonsai trees or anything else that's commonly gossiped about by the water cooler in the office.

Here's an example of how in-jokes work in a business context. As expected, these aren't very funny if you don't know the circumstances and people involved. But because everyone in this audience knew the characters referred to very well, the seemingly mild gags brought the house down. The occasion was a business conference for a large UK telecommunications corporation.

> **Flight attendant 1:** *Good morning/afternoon ladies and gentlemen. On behalf of Captain XXX and his crew we'd like to welcome you aboard this British Teleways flight 2002 to ICT Solution Sales Training – our fantastic new destination channel that's going to be a* real *winner with all our passengers next year.*

As this is our maiden flight to the new destination you'll be pleased to hear that our in-flight entertainment today is all live and all performed by female flight attendants.

Flight attendant 2: *It's for this reason that the two Senior Captains who should have been travelling with us today were especially disappointed not to be on the flight after all. They of course are Captain Peter YYY who reluctantly decided to take himself by sea – and Captain Phil ZZZ who is flying at 30,000 feet anyway, now that Wolverhampton Wanderers have finally got to the top of the 1st Division.*

Now let's take a look at how the in-jokes concept can work for a social occasion. The following are excerpts from speeches I wrote for a bar mitzvah. The first is by the bar mitzvah boy's 16-year-old brother, and the second by the (13 year old) bar mitzvah boy himself. I spent about a week on and off with this family getting to know their personalities and in-jokes and it paid off. They and their 350 guests thought the speeches were fantastic. Mind you they all knew the boys and their personalities really well. Just for fun, see how much you can gather about their personalities from the in-jokes I've used for them.

Older brother: *Good evening. I'd like to spend the next few minutes talking to you about XXX.*

It started way back when he appeared as a cute little baby. Apart from our parents that's the only thing we've ever had in common.

But we're so different, I think my parents probably brought him home from a maternity clinic on another planet.

Take food, for example. Whereas I'm a bit picky and enjoy the finer culinary delights ... with XXX, you could serve him a plate of roasted football boots and he'd eat it. As long as there was lots of it and plenty of ketchup. And of course, he doesn't share. He hoards food like it's going out of fashion. I like to make my Mum her favourite snack when she's up in the office working late. XXX might think of doing that but he'd eat it himself on the way upstairs.

Now ... clothes. Everybody jokes about the fact I like Gucci and Prada, but after all, I am the son of a fashion-conscious family. But the closest XXX's ever come to being label conscious, is knowing the difference between Arsenal home and away shirts. And that's when he's going somewhere special. The rest of the time he's so badly dressed even the dog won't be seen out with him.

Being tidy is another thing. OK, I admit it. I'm not tidy. Well, I'm the creative type. But XXX's so obsessed with neatness and regularity, he'd drive an accountant to distraction. He even makes his bed in the morning half asleep as the alarm's going off, before he's even finished getting out of it.

Then, there's preparations. I tend to make mine for things at the last minute, when it's all fresh in my mind. But even when he's just getting ready for school, XXX's got to have everything laid out like it was morning drill in an

Army boot camp. Sometimes I wonder why he even bothers to go to bed. If he didn't he could then use the whole night to get ready for school.

Sport is another thing. My idea of good sport is something with a bit of class, you know, backgammon or chess. But XXX's out there every weekend running after a ball in six inches of mud. At least that David Beckham manages to dress reasonably well. That's amazing considering he's depriving some village of an idiot. Perhaps that's why he plays for Arsenal.

Younger brother *(Bar mitzvah boy): ... YYY is pretty strong as well. But I'm getting stronger and can deck him in a double armlock any time I like. I know he complains that I don't share with him. I don't understand it. I've offered to share a lot of my things with him but he's not interested. Not my hoards of chocolate biscuits, Westlife CDs, dirty football kit, nothing.*

It's all very well for him to laugh at me taking plenty of time to get ready for school. But I think that's a lot better than his way ... being shouted at eight times to make his bed ... and leaving everything so late he's running out to the car still trying to do up his trousers.

And as for all this fashion stuff ... well, YYY, I know David Beckham wears lots of Gucci and Prada. (Sarcastically) *And that says a lot for Beckham's brain power, doesn't it?*

Anyway if YYY was going to play any games at all, they'd be with Mrs Beckham, wouldn't they!

Well, maybe YYY and I did come from different planets. On the other hand, we orbit around the same thing – our family.

Okay, we're really different, but we're both loyal players on the ZZZ team. Actually I couldn't wish for a better brother. Nobody else could argue so well.

'In-jokes' for wedding speeches: yes, but ...

We can all be forgiven for thinking that in-jokes such as those I've shown above would work well for a wedding speech. Well, the answer is yes, but...

It all comes back to my earlier point about really understanding your audience.

One wonderful thing about marriage is that often it brings two entirely different families – two entirely different groups of people – together. But that's where a problem can begin if you tell in-jokes; one half of the audience will find them hilarious while the other half doesn't begin to understand what you're talking about.

And don't forget, even if the audience at a wedding is relatively small, it can still comprise a surprisingly wide range of people in terms of age, cultural/ethnic background, and so on.

My advice is, only tell in-jokes if one or more of the following apply:

◆ both families come from the same community/ethnic group

◆ both family/social groups have known each other for a long time, very well

◆ you know the whole audience (possibly a small one) is closely acquainted with both bride and groom.

And now don't forget, there is more to life than humour. How about poetry?

Poetry – How to Use It Creatively

You will probably be amused to know that in researching for this book I have spent over a week slaving over my computer and various books all in the quest of some simple answers to this question: 'What's the easy way to write poetry?'

The short answer is, 'there isn't one'. Not because writing poetry has to be difficult and complex, but simply because, it turns out, poetry today can be pretty much anything you like from a perfectly crafted Shakespearean sonnet to three lines all consisting of identical words.

In short, poetry is words with rhythm however you like 'em. They don't even have to rhyme.

As I see it (but I'm no poet, believe me) the art of poetry lies in its 'marriage' (sorry!) between pleasing sound patterns created by the words, and a distinct message created by the thinking behind the words. This is what makes it such an attractive element of a wedding speech.

YOU CAN WRITE AN ORIGINAL POEM

If you want to use some poetry in your speech forget trying to compete with Wordsworth or Keats; if you want to quote poetry of that type and standard then just help yourself to it. Unless you just so happen to be an accomplished poet yourself, an original poem of your own will be much more effective is it's kept simple and uncomplicated.

Let's see, without becoming intellectually stressed, how to put some simple poetry together that will contribute cleverly to your wedding speech.

A very brief word about technicalities

As I said, poems these days don't even need to rhyme. However, if they're going to work they need to adhere to some sort of rhythm pattern. And if you're a bit of a traditionalist like me you will probably prefer to make the odd few lines, at least, rhyme in that old-fashioned way.

I won't even go near the proper technical terms of poetry here, but if you want to learn more about them I have included some references in the resources section at the back of this book. Here, though, are some very basic tips to bear in mind.

Pick a rhythm for your poem and try to stick to it as closely as possible

Define this to yourself by using the sounds 'de DUM de DUM,' etc. So the first stanza of a simple poem would be worked out like this:

Some	mot	or	ists	are	ve	ry	kind
de	*DUM*	*de*	*DUM*	*de*	*DUM*	*de*	*DUM*
To	hors	es	some	what	heat	ed	
de	*DUM*	*de*	*DUM*	*de*	*de*	*de*	
You	slow	and	stop,	with	eng	ines	off,
de	*DUM*	*de*	*DUM*	*de*	*DUM*	*de*	*DUM*
So	we	can	re	main	seat	ed.	
de	*DUM*	*de*	*DUM*	*de*	*de*	*de*	

This gives you the basic rhythmic structure you need to work from.

Decide which lines should rhyme

In the case of the poem above, it's lines number two and four that rhyme. The way to remember that – and the fact that lines one and three don't rhyme – is: A – B – C – B.

Probably the form I've used here is the easiest, but if you're feeling ambitious you can use pretty well any combination of rhyming scheme you like. Another common form is A – B – A – B, which means that rhymes occur with lines one and three and lines two and four. You could also choose A – A – B – B, etc.

Think of a theme, an idea, a story

As we know, poems are a combination of nice sounding, rhythmic words with a message. It's very easy for the inexperienced poet to get that balance wrong and tend to focus more on the rhythm and rhyme of the words themselves than on what they're actually *saying*.

So think of what you want your poem to *say*. It could be about:

♦ this wedding day
♦ your own marriage
♦ your relationship with the bride and/or groom
♦ your views on love
♦ your love for your children.

As always, some tasteful humour works well here and you may want to introduce some into your poem. This does not have to run wall-to-wall; there is no reason why some verses of your poem can't be serious while others are funny.

Make a list of useful rhyming words

Think of some key words to express your theme or story, then list as many words as you can think of that rhyme with them. Don't forget words that begin with more than one consonant, that are multi-syllabic, etc. Let's say you want to write an amusing short poem about your grandson, the bridegroom, whose name is Will. Here's the list of words you might put down.

Will	love	Gran	groom
bill	above	Nan	boom
fill	dove	man	loom
hill	glove	ban	broom
mill	'guv'	can	room
until	of	fan	bedroom

... and so-on. You may not use all or even any of these, but it helps to give you some guidelines. Also check out Resources, pages 205–6 for rhyming dictionaries and similar online resources.

Decide how many verses you want and allocate a 'task' to each one

In other words, you should try to plan your poem out as far as you can. Bearing in mind that you may be a little restrained by finding words that fit in with the rhythm *and* rhyme with each other, you may want to allow yourself to be a bit flexible here.

So your poem plan for this same example might be

- Stanza 1: Will when he was little.
- Stanza 2: Will growing up.
- Stanza 3: Will as a soldier in the Army.
- Stanza 4: Will as a married man.

And off you go start writing!

To give you a little something to help get the creative flow going, here is a poem I wrote one day after a ride on my horse when the horse had been frightened by the loud noise of the air brakes letting off from a lorry which had kindly stopped to let us go by safely. Lorry drivers, nice though their intentions are, don't seem to realise that once the horse is adjacent to the back of the lorry it's right by those noisy brakes. And horses hate hissing noises. (Excerpted from my *The Horse Lover's Joke Book*, Kenilworth Press, 2001.)

Ode to Motorists in Country Lanes

Some motorists are very kind
To horses somewhat heated
You slow and stop, with engines off,
So we can remain seated.

The trouble is once we have gone
Beyond your line of vision
You fire your engine, roaring loud
With racing-start precision.

Creating thus some equine fear
Your clutch engages, wallop!
Your tyres bite on verge and grit
Then horse goes into gallop.

And lorry drivers, you're the best
At seeing us fast departed.
If when we're feet from a lorry's rear
Your airbrakes have just f*rted.

So though we're grateful for the thought
From all you careful drivers
Please wait till we are truly past
Or you'll need to revive us.

Jo Parfitt, a great friend and colleague of mine wrote a poem for her own wedding speech and has shared her personal tips with us here.

WRITING YOUR OWN WEDDING POEM
Some notes by JO PARFITT

Scanning is important. Always tum-te-tum it out to see if it scans nicely. Look for patterns in the rhymes either at the ends of lines or within lines. For example:

I'd always poo-pooed the idea that once wooed

Or

It's rare that an ungainly goose
Can trap a man without a noose

I like to have different patterns that may seem random but work fine when read aloud.

With my poem, the rhyme scheme evolved to match the words which ran something like this

> I'd always poo-pooed the idea that once wooed
> I'd jack in my job for a bloke
> But now it's occurred, my career's been deferred
> And my jetset idea's up in smoke.

> It's rare that an ungainly goose,
> Can trap a man without a noose,
> Make him chuck away his wetsuit
> Fling away his fins
> Discard his trusty depth-gauge

And unstring his violin
For the ordinary life
Of married man with quacking wife!

... etc.

Note the word ordinary I pronounced this oR–diN-air-Y to make it fit the scan scheme better.

My advice is go for laughs. Remember it is to be read aloud, so keep it short and snappy. Use puns and plays on words. However *avoid* cheap rhymes and sentence constructions like:

I've known Jonathan for many a year
and his snoring is terrible I do hear

Short lines and frequent rhymes work better:

I've known that for ages
Jon's kept rats in cages

Jo Parfitt, The Book Cook,
www.summertimepublishing.com

LIMERICKS: AN EXCELLENT CHOICE FOR WEDDINGS

Limericks are all-time favourites for light-hearted, happy occasions and are surprisingly easy to write. Because of their well-known structure and strong connections with the naughty world of adult humour audiences will tend to assume a limerick is going to be funny as soon as you start reading or reciting it.

Also, limericks only have to be vaguely connected with the person or occasion at which they are performed, and in some ways the more outrageous and/or silly they are the more the audience will appreciate them.

The rhythm of a limerick is always basically the same, although you can add little twiddles to it such as those I have included in brackets:

1. *De DUM de de DUM de de DUM (de)*
2. *De DUM de de DUM de de DUM (de)*
3. *De de DUM de de DUM (de)*
4. *De de DUM de de DUM (de)*
5. *De DUM de de DUM de de DUM (de)*

And the rhyming scheme of a limerick is always the same, too; lines one, two and five rhyme with each other, and lines three and four rhyme with each other. So, for the record, the pattern goes A-A-B-B-A.

The trick when writing limericks is to pick line-end words that offer you lots of rhyming options. The other day a friend was going to a birthday party where every guest had to get up and perform a limerick about the birthday boy, a lawyer whose name was a very useful 'Tim.' This is what I wrote for my friend to say:

There was a smart lawyer called Tim
Who never quite learned how to swim
But a plaintiff from hell
Threw him into a well
Now Tim's back-stroke's superbly in trim.

I think my job would have been harder if the lawyer's name had been, say, Marcus or Boris!

As with other types of poetry it's a great help if you decide on your theme – which is nearly always expressed in the first line of the limerick – and then list as many words that rhyme with the line-end word of your choice. This gives you a range to choose from for lines one, two and five. In the case of Tim, here, I wrote down the following:

> Tim, dim, him, Jim, gym, Kim, limb,
> rim, vim, whim, slim, swim, trim

I liked the idea of 'swim' so it wasn't hard to come up with the idea for lines three and four. And the last line needs a bit of punch, and/or to create a surprise – it's like the punchline of a joke.

ADAPTING EXISTING POETIC MATERIAL

If you don't want to write your own poem from scratch, you could consider adapting some well known material for the purposes of your wedding speech.

This does not necessarily have to be a poem; it can be the words of a song, a hymn, or even a prayer. And any lawyers reading this book please calm down. I honestly don't think anyone would ever complain about someone reciting the words to a copyrighted piece at a private event like a wedding. In any case a great deal of popular, well known poems, songs and hymns are either out of copyright or not subject to copyright laws anyway.

Let's be naughty for a moment then and look at how we could use some of that old Cahn/Van Heusen song made famous by Frank Sinatra, called *Love and Marriage*.

Original:
Love and marriage, love and marriage
Go together like a horse and carriage
This I tell you brother
You can't have one, you can't have one, you can't have one without the other

Now – in your role as sister or mother of the bridegroom, whose name is Simon:

Your potential adaptation:
Love and marriage, love and marriage
Go together like a horse and carriage
This I tell you, Simon
So you beware, you'll get nowhere, unless you really put the time in!

REWRITTEN NURSERY RHYMES
Another type of poem/song you might like to adapt is the nursery rhyme. Here are some examples from two of my joke books, to give you a flavour of how these can work.

Little Miss Whippet
Was no more than a snippet
Sniffing the curds and whey
When along came a spider
Started eating beside her

'I'll teach him,' she thought, 'right away.'
So little Miss Whippet
Despite being a snippet
Stood up and started to squeal
The spider was shock-ed
Took off like a rocket
And Miss Whippet partook of the meal.
(Excerpted from *Canine Capers*, Kenilworth Press, 2002)

Little Miss Maddle
Sat in the saddle
Eating her Burger King
When came a bike rider
That revved up beside her
And her horse began fast galloping
Poor Little Miss Maddle
Fell out of the saddle
Straight on to her safety hat
Still clutching her burger
Her shouts threatened murder
'Now I can't have my french fries with that!'
(Excerpted from *The Horse Lover's Joke Book*, Kenilworth Press, 2001)

Jack and Jill went up the hill
To fetch their dog some water
But when they returned the dog was concerned
With guzzling their nice bread and bawt-ter.
(Excerpted from *Canine Capers*, Kenilworth Press, 2002)

Jack and Jill went up the hill
To try to jump the water
Jack made a hash and fell with a splash
But Jill jumped clear as one oughta.
(Excerpted from *The Horse Lover's Joke Book*, Kenilworth Press, 2001)

Mary had a little pup
Its teeth were sharp as razors
And everywhere that Mary went
It tore things up to blazes.
(Excerpted from *Canine Capers*, Kenilworth Press, 2002)

Mary had a little horse
Which kicked like there's no tomorrow
And everywhere that Mary went
No other horse dared follow
(Excerpted from *The Horse Lover's Joke Book*, Kenilworth Press, 2001)

Mary Mary quite contrary
How was obedience class?
Sit and stay went quite well but his 'walkies' were hell
Barbara Woodhouse, your methods were crass.
(Excerpted from *Canine Capers*, Kenilworth Press, 2002)

Mary Mary quite contrary
How did the dressage test go?
Counter-canter went well but my half-pass was hell
So in all it was quite a poor show.
(Excerpted from *The Horse Lover's Joke Book*, Kenilworth Press 2001)

Little Bo-Peep has lost her sheep
And she's no idea where to find them
The sheepdog got wind of a bitch and some sin
So ran off and left her to mind them
(Excerpted from *Canine Capers*, Kenilworth Press, 2002)

Little Bo-Porse got bucked off her horse
And she's no idea where to find him
Leave him alone, he'll make his way home
Trailing his reins behind him
(Excerpted from *The Horse Lover's Joke Book*, Kenilworth Press, 2001)

Happy poetry writing!

Rehearsal and Delivery: Putting Your Money Where Your Mouth Is

I don't want to make you feel depressed, but once you've finished all the hard work of researching, preparing your material and writing your speech you then get down to the really hard work – rehearsing.

Some people advocate the impromptu speech, especially for weddings and other social occasions. As long as you have a few minutes beforehand to gather your thoughts and scribble a few notes, they say, you'll be fine.

And in some cases, chances are they're right. But on an occasion as important as your wedding (or that of someone you're very close to) who needs to leave it to chance? Blame it on my being a boring old Taurean if you like, but I do not support that view unless you happen to be a very practised, accomplished public speaker in the first place. And if you were, you probably wouldn't be reading this book.

PRACTICE MAKES PERFECT AND ALL THAT

So – you've got to practise, practise, practise. Not too soon before the event, or you'll be so stale and fed up with the speech you'll lose interest. But don't wait until the last minute, either. Just as was the case with your GCSEs and other school exams, swatting up whatever you can the night before is unlikely to bring you much success.

Memorise the speech as well as you can, but don't worry if you forget the odd 'and' or 'but'. If you say 'er' and hesitate slightly now and again, it will make your speech sound more natural. What you must memorise perfectly is the content, and the order.

Then on the day, you will use your script or bullet points as a reminder – not as an essential element that you would be desperate without. All that rehearsal – in the shower, in the car, to your family or if they don't appreciate your oratory, even to your dog – will pay off because you will be confident, and that's because:

1. Your material is good.
2. You know it well.

WORKING WITH AN AUDIO RECORDER

Some people find working with an audio recorder quite a useful way to practise a speech. Simply record yourself reading it into your recorder and then play it back to yourself, speaking it along with your own voice. It's something you can do at home or in your car and even on the bus or train, although that might get you some funny looks from fellow passengers!

The other benefit of using the audio recorder is that by listening to yourself say your speech, you'll notice any areas where you tend to stumble over a word, where a sentence doesn't work as you had intended, where a joke falls a bit flat, etc. This gives you the opportunity to polish your speech. However, don't make the mistake of making radical changes at the last minute, unless of course unexpected events force you to do so.

Now, enough from a mere speech-writer. While researching for this book I was lucky enough to interview Gail Cornish LNEA. Gail is a drama teacher at the acclaimed Artists' Theatre School in London (*www.artiststheatreschool.com*) and she kindly took time out to give us her advice. It's incredibly helpful – so enjoy!

Here's how our conversation went.

INTERVIEW WITH GAIL CORNISH LNEA, DRAMA TEACHER

Part One, rehearsal and practising

**Gail ... now, obviously the majority of women reading this book will not be professional actors or presenters, so please bear that in mind! First of all, compared with a man's voice, how does a woman's voice travel and project to an audience? What disadvantages does she have from this point of view?

Any advantages?

A woman's voice tends to travel and project better than a man's because it is lighter and higher. However, this can tend to give her less 'authority' when speaking.

**What can a 'lay' female speaker do to improve the way her voice sounds when speaking to an audience?

An untrained female speaker should concentrate on keeping her voice as low in pitch as possible (without sounding Margaret Thatcherish!) to avoid any shrillness.

**When she is practising her speech, what exercises could she do to improve her voice quality and projection/volume?

When practising her speech, she should do breathing exercises (the breath is the 'petrol', so to speak, for the voice engine – most people breathe too shallowly), facial warm up exercises, vocal warm up exercises (see below) *and practise speaking to the end of a room, to the end of the garden, speaking while the radio is playing – all of these can help to keep the volume up. Also practise speaking slowly. Record yourself doing the speech – you will probably be speaking too fast. Go at half the speed that you think feels right – then halve it again – that will probably be about right for public speaking!*

**Any other tips?

Practise status: say the speech with your toes turned inward, your shoulders hunched, looking down or flicking your eyes around, touching your face and hair frequently. Then drop all those behaviours. Say the speech standing straight, looking straight ahead and sweeping your eyes slowly around from one side to the other, keeping your hands and head straight and still.

Find (or create – StM) places in the speech where you can breathe deeply and slowly. Practise saying the speech slowly, exaggerating the breath marks.

Another helpful way to prepare for your speech is to use visualisation techniques. In the following excerpt from Philip Calvert's top-selling book, *Make A Great Wedding Speech* (How To Books) Philip kindly shares with us the technique of 'seeing' our way to success.

VISUALISE YOURSELF DELIVERING A GREAT SPEECH

Now, I'm no expert on the inner workings of wonders of the human mind, but what I do know is that a superb way of rehearsing your speech is to do it 'in your head'. In fact, running through your speech in your mind can often be as effective a rehearsal as doing it for real.

The subconscious mind can't tell the difference between something that is real or something that is vividly imagined. If you vividly imagine yourself delivering your speech with confidence, flair, style, good humour and warmth, your execution on the day itself will reflect this because your mind will believe that it has had a 'real' rehearsal ...

... Unlike real rehearsals, you can do these mental practice sessions as often as you want. And every session will be of benefit however short.

Tips on visualisation rehearsals

◆ Start by vividly imagining how you will feel as you sit down after giving your speech.

◆ Make a conscious effort to imagine what it will be like and how good you will feel as all the guests applaud loudly and enthusiastically.

◆ Imagine several people patting you firmly on the back as they congratulate you and others giving you the thumbs up from tables across the room.

◆ See their faces as they tell you what a great speech it was. Listen to the words they use and feel yourself smiling broadly and being proud of your fantastic achievement.

◆ Now rewind this 'film' in your mind to the start of your speech and see yourself rising to your feet.

◆ You feel relaxed, confident and are looking forward to talking to the guests. You already know that they are going to enjoy your speech and will applaud loudly.

◆ See and hear yourself speaking in your mind's eye. See yourself looking guests in the eye and feel the warmth of their response in return.

◆ See the guests nodding, smiling and enjoying themselves and imagine how that will make you feel.

Come the moment of truth, you will be amazed at how what you imagined beforehand magically comes to life. In short, creative visualisation is a superb tool for both building your confidence and getting vital rehearsal time.

And now, on to the day itself ... delivery.

First of all, the second half of our interview with Gail Cornish.

INTERVIEW WITH GAIL CORNISH LNEA, DRAMA TEACHER

Part Two, warming up and delivery

**What tips have you got to help the woman relax and 'warm up' before she speaks (given that she won't be in a dressing room but probably sitting at the head table in front of everyone else!)

To relax and warm up before the speech, while sitting on the dais: relax your hands in your lap, if you can surreptitiously stretch them fully and let them fall loose a couple of times. Then breathe right down into your diaphragm for the count of three, hold the breath for the count of three, and breathe out through your lips for a count of four. Do the same, breathing out for a count of five, then six, then seven and so on, as much as you can do. This helps calm the nerves as well as filling your lungs and getting the blood circulating.

**What advice would you give to our woman speaker about body language in front of the audience?

Keep as still as possible. Keep head and hands as still as possible. When making a speech, you are high status – high status people keep still. Make eye contact with the audience, sweeping your eyes slowly around to encompass everybody. Make eye contact with a specific area of the audience when making an important point. Be sure to do this with different areas of the audience at various times, so that everyone feels included.

**What advice would you give her about the way she speaks when delivering her speech?

Slow down! Nerves, breathlessness, stumbling over words, forgetting where you are in the speech, all result in people speaking faster and faster – which, of course, makes the whole thing worse. You almost cannot speak too slowly when making a speech.

**Are there any additional tips from the theatre world you can add to help get over nerves, improve her confidence, etc.?

Tips from the theatre – that's a laugh, since many actors hate making speeches and are terrible at it! The breathing exercise I mentioned earlier is very good.

Also: breathe in through your nose for the count of three, hold for the count of three, breathe out through your mouth in little puffs as if blowing out a candle for the count of four, then five, then six, etc.

**And what if our speaker can escape to the ladies' room for a few minutes before the speeches start?

Do facial exercises: Stretch your face as wide and high as it can go, then scrunch it up as tight as you can. Do this several times, getting quicker each time.

Stick your tongue out as far as it will go – try to touch your nose, chin, left ear, right ear (with your tongue, of course!)

Make rapid blabblabblabbla noises with your tongue, also 'rrrrrr', rolling the 'r'. Blow raspberries through your lips, also 'horses blowing' noises, also kissing. And yawn.

Say: 'I can make my voice go higher and higher' and 'I can make my voice go lower and lower', going higher as you say the first and lower as you say the second.

Say tongue twisters: 'Red lorry yellow lorry', 'red leather yellow leather', 'the Leith police dismisseth us', 'imagine managing an imaginary menagerie' are all good ones as you can't say them properly without a mobile face and lips and tongue. All of these will help with producing words clearly and voice projection.

If you are reading the speech, hold the paper away from your face, fairly low, and speak the first half dozen words direct to the audience before looking down for the next bit.

**And lastly most importantly?

Smile!

Gail, thank you so much!

DELIVERY TIPS: MY OWN, FOR WHAT THEY'RE WORTH!

As you may have gathered from the terrific input from other people in this chapter I'm no expert on delivery and presentation techniques. That's because I'm a speechwriter, so content is my real forté.

Having said that I have worked with professional, amateur and social speakers extensively over the last, well, I won't admit how many years! And over that time I have learned not just how to write for them but also how to help them develop their presentation and delivery performances.

Often I've ended up stage directing speakers, usually because the actual director was held up in traffic or otherwise distracted. But I never turned down an opportunity to help rehearse and direct speakers on stage because of the chance it gave me to learn about disciplines other than my own, and to get a better view of my own skills in the broader context.

In fact, I have given speeches. Many times. I won't bore you with why, where and how, but suffice it to say many of those occasions have been – once again – when the proper person was otherwise indisposed, drunk, petrified from stage fright, under the influence of recreational drugs, being sick as a result of pregnancy, plus a whole host of reasons not suitable for a family audience. The net result, though, was that I have served my apprenticeship as a speaker as well as writer, despite never (so far) having spoken at a wedding.

So without boring you further, I know how it feels! And despite having to bow to the far greater expertise of Gail, Phil, Simon et

al who have contributed to this chapter, here are my own few tips
and observations on how to get the best from your presentation
and delivery.

BEFORE YOU GIVE YOUR SPEECH

Forget about 'Dutch courage' – don't drink any alcohol until
after you've given your speech. In my many years of writing
speeches for business people and social speakers I've heard all the
rationales about a drink or two loosening the tongue, calming
your nerves, relaxing you, making you funnier, etc., and they're all
bullsh*t. Even one drink affects your concentration detrimentally
and can ruin your performance.

If you can't escape somewhere private to practise Gail's facial and
vocal exercises, go into a quiet corner and pout as hard as you
can, then release your lips. Grimace, then relax. Do this a few
times. It will help relax your facial muscles and help you speak
more easily.

MICROPHONES: HOW TO USE THEM

If a microphone is available, take advantage of it – don't be
afraid of it! Usually a microphone at a wedding will be on a
stand, either a table stand or a full stand depending on the set-up.
If you are the first speaker to go you'll need to check if the
microphone is live; this you do by tapping it gently with your
finger. Whatever you do don't blow down it as the moisture from
your breath can damage its innards. If it isn't live check that it's
switched on; usually the on-off switch is on the side of the device,
or sometimes at the bottom.

Assuming you haven't had the chance to do an on-site rehearsal, use your first line as the test to see where you should position the mike and yourself to get the best effect. Don't worry if you need to fiddle with it for a moment or two – there's no meter running, so take your time. If you're not the first speaker to go you shouldn't have to make anything other than very minor adjustments to the mike, but if you are the first it may take a bit of trial and error.

Then, when you're speaking, make sure that wherever you are – and you may be moving around a little to look at your audience (see below) – the microphone is more or less directly between you and the audience. In other words, 'aim' your voice so it goes towards the microphone first, as I've attempted to illustrate below. First of all, looking straight ahead:

> **Looking at**
> **audience here**
>
> **Microphone**
>
> **You here**

Then, to your left.

> **Looking at**
> **audience here**
>
> **Microphone**
>
> **You here**

And finally to your right.

> **Looking at
> audience here**
>
> **Microphone**
>
> **You here**

You don't need to move very much to achieve this – probably a matter of inches. However if you don't move appropriately, as in this diagram:

> **Looking at
> audience here**
>
> **Microphone**
>
> **You here**

your voice will go past the microphone and not get picked up properly. People will tell you not to worry about this as the microphone is omni-directional and can pick up a fly's footsteps at a distance of 20 metres. Don't listen to them. Even an omni-directional mike may go quiet on you unless you aim your voice squarely at it.

Finally, remember not to rely on a microphone too much. Even with electronic help you still need to speak out and project your voice when you're giving a speech. A quiet mutter will still sound like a quiet mutter whether amplified or not.

SOME MORE OF MY TIPS

◆ Stand up proudly – shoulders back. This give you more authority and makes people take notice.

◆ When you look around to get eye contact with people, keep moving your eyeline around but not too quickly or you'll look shifty. If your audience is large, split the room visually into sections and then look at each section in turn.

◆ My grandfather had a lovely saying ... 'smile when you don't feel like it, and you will feel like it when you smile'. Smile when you're talking even if you're nervous. It's infectious – people will smile with you. And if you're smiling you won't look nervous, even if you are.

◆ Try to keep your hands still, either by your sides or resting on the table or lectern. If you want, use one hand to gesture and emphasise what you're saying, but be careful that this doesn't look contrived. (A few practice sessions in the bathroom mirror are worth considering.)

◆ If you fluff a line or mess something up, don't apologise. Just smile and keep going.

◆ If you feel nervous, remember that's natural and if anything, it's good. The extra adrenaline pumping around in your system will help keep you on your toes mentally.

AND IF YOU'RE STILL NERVOUS ...

If you're still feeling nervous about giving your speech on the day, here is another great idea from my very kind team of contributing experts. This tip is excerpted from the eBook *Like A Brick Wrapped In Velvet* by Dr Simon Raybould of Curved Vision, the specialist consultancy that uses the techniques of professional theatre in the 'real' world (*www.curved-vision.co.uk*). Simon's original version is very detailed, but bearing in mind that my word count for this book was limited I have edited it to fit. The original version appears in Simon's eBook and is available from the Curved Vision website.

ANCHORING

Anchoring is a term used heavily in NLP (Neuro Linguistic Programming). Essentially it's a process of associating being relaxed and confident with ... well ... almost anything, really!

Anyone who has heard their school drama teachers saying something like 'do it just like you did in rehearsals and you'll be great' has heard a crude form of anchoring being used. Here, the teacher is trying to get the pupils to forget their nerves by remembering how well and how confidently they ran through the play (or dance, or whatever) when they were rehearsing it.

A much more effective version of this technique is to establish some kind of semi-formal routine, or ritual. This ritual must be something you do every time you practise, so that by doing it again before you perform live your subconscious brain automatically associates what your body is currently doing with how it felt last time you did your ritual – at rehearsals perhaps, when you were relaxed, confident, and knew that if you made a mistake you could just deal with it and go on.

Perhaps an example will serve to illustrate the point better:

> 'I'm married and I wear a platinum ring. For me, the ring is associated with many of the good things in my life. Because my wedding ring represents that, touching it reminds me of that. For a while, I made a point of rotating it by 45° with the thumb of my left hand every time I walked up the path to my front door. After I'd done that for a while, whenever I rotated my ring, it reminded me of arriving home and how much more relaxed and secure I felt as I got there. Now, when I'm nervous, I simply rotate the ring and all the good feelings of home come instantly to mind. It sounds too simple to be true but the effects can be quite remarkable.'

When you decide to 'anchor' your confident state to something, use a bit of common sense and the following points to guide you:

- Don't pick on an object *(other than, like the person above, a wedding or other ring you never take off – StM)* stick to an action or something that is absolutely guaranteed to be with you always.
- Pick something that is easy to do, not a complicated routine.
- Choose something that's not obtrusive so you can do it without people noticing.
- Pick something unusual, not something you do frequently already.
- You need to do it *whenever* you practise.

- It's possible to combine this anchor with, say, a breathing exercise.

And finally, here's a very encouraging quote from John Bowden's excellent book, *Making The Best Man's Speech* (How To Books) which applies every bit as much to your speech as it does to all the others.

The audience is on your side. They are willing you to do well and, quite frankly, they won't give a damn if you fluff a line or two. What they *will* mind, though, is if it becomes embarrassingly obvious that you have not even bothered to take the time or effort to find out what is expected of you.

Enough said! By now you should be feeling much more confident that you're thoroughly capable of researching, preparing, rehearsing and delivering the wedding speech of a lifetime. So all that's left is to determine what to talk about.

Part 2

Developing Your Content

HOW TO USE THIS BOOK TO CREATE YOUR SPEECH

I debated long and hard whether to include some sample speeches in this book. Then I had a look on the internet and found hundreds upon hundreds of them, freely available from websites. I read – well, not hundreds, but – several dozen and thought they were all awful. Not because they were badly written, you understand, but because they were written either for an imaginary speaker or for someone else, nothing to do with you or me.

I think it's far better to move straight on to *your* speech. Not only will that result in a better presentation, but it will feel absolutely right for you. (Think of it as the difference between 'off-the-peg' and 'haute couture' fashion.) Here is how to do it.

♦ Read Chapter 2 and understand the method that uses these steps:
  1. Create bullet points of the basic things you want to say.
  2. Add scribbled notes to those bullets.
  3. Put all that into a logical order – add more notes if you want.
  4. Talk around the bullets and notes into an audio recorder.
  5. Transcribe that, which results in your rough script.

♦ Turn to Part 2 of the book and find the chapter that matches (as closely as possible) your speaking role at the wedding.

♦ Run through the 'Content Idea Triggers' section and have a good think about how those ideas can be applied to your personal circumstances.

♦ Carry out steps 1 and 2.

♦ Move on to the section of the chapter called 'Your Structure Skeleton'. Use the ideas and options here to help you carry out step 3.

♦ Now put this book down and carry out steps 4 and 5.

♦ Get the book out again and turn to the second half of Chapter 2. From here through to the end of Chapter 4, you'll find some useful help to create the finer details of your speech.

♦ Also use Part 3 of the book as a back-up for resources of jokes, poetry, quotations, etc.

(If you would like to have a look at some ready-made sample speeches all the same, in the back of the book I have included some resources you can look up.)

SPEECHES FOR CIVIL PARTNERSHIP CELEBRATIONS

As I'm writing this book, Civil Partnership legislation is just becoming live in the UK. By the time *Wedding Speeches For Women* is in the bookshops and in your hands, many Civil Partnership ceremonies will have taken place already and many more will be planned.

Although at first glance it may seem wrong of me not to include material directly relevant to women giving speeches at Civil Partnership celebrations, I do have what I think is a good reason. This is, quite simply, that in my view any such occasion is a union between two people who love each other, whatever it's called. The politicians and civil servants might argue over differences, but for our purposes these are very, very few. Consequently, all but perhaps occasional sentences in this book are as relevant to Civil Partnership celebrations as they are to 'weddings' across the board.

Obviously if you are a lesbian you will be aware of any issues both negative and positive (like humour for example) that you need to bear in mind when giving a speech at a gay or lesbian wedding. And I assume that if you are not a lesbian but are asked to give a speech at a gay or lesbian wedding, you are very close to one or both partners concerned so you are also likely to know of such issues.

If you bear those issues in mind when planning and preparing your speech and address them with empathy, humour and love, you won't go wrong.

'Traditional Male' Speeches and How to Replace Them

Strictly speaking there's nothing special about traditional speeches given by the father of the bride or by the best man. What can make it special in our case is that the speech concerned is given by a woman.

Now, you and the rest of the bridal party may decide to dispense with tradition altogether and make speeches about whatever you feel like. In that case, skip the next few pages. But although you may break with tradition in some ways, there are a few inescapable necessities in wedding speeches which are pure good manners and courtesy, whoever says them. Let's take another look at these two traditional roles and see what within those you can safely ignore, and what you should retain.

- ◆ **The father of the bride (or other close male relative of hers, or sometimes an old family friend)**
  He talks about the bride – usually makes her squirm with embarrassment at the anecdotes of the bride aged five with her teddy bears and dolls! He welcomes the guests to the wedding and the groom and his family into his own. He will also thank people for their efforts in the wedding preparations (especially the bride's mother, if appropriate) and mention special guests who can't be present. Finally he proposes a toast to the bride and groom.

- ◆ **The best man**
  He thanks the bridegroom for his speech and – on behalf of the bridal attendants – for his toast. He talks about the groom, and his relationship with him. He then reads out any telemessages and cards that have accumulated, and ends by proposing a toast to the bride and groom.

Okay, let's be horribly unromantic for a bit and analyse those speeches into individual chunks and how you, as the speech-maker replacing the bride's father or the best man, can regard the content within your own speech. Please note that you may find some helpful ideas in the chapters that follow – they're well worth checking out, even if your content is constrained to the conventional.

IF YOU'RE SPEAKING INSTEAD OF THE FATHER OF THE BRIDE

Here's how we can break down the elements of the traditional 'father of the bride' speech and see how each one should or should not be included in yours.

Content 'idea triggers'

◆ *Talks about the bride – **Yes***
This should be retained in your speech. Even in these equality-driven days this is more her day than anyone else's and it's one she will remember for the rest of her life. As 'another woman' you may not have quite the close, cuddly relationship with the bride that her Daddy would, but in many ways this can be a good thing. You, as another woman, will probably be able to sing her praises and underline her qualities in a way that Daddy never could, expressing genuine admiration without being overly sentimental (see below).

◆ *Usually makes her squirm with embarrassment at the anecdotes of the bride aged five with her teddy bears and dolls! – **No***
Or a least, probably not, unless you can do it without making the poor girl's teeth grind. There's a big difference between amusing anecdotes about someone's youth and a long eulogy about changing her nappies. Daddies can sometimes get this one hideously wrong, especially if they have had a few alcoholic snifters by the time we get to the speeches. You, as a sensible woman, know the difference between speech content that makes everyone smile nostalgically, including the bride, and the other variety.

◆ *Welcomes the guests to the wedding – **Yes***
This one depends a little on where in the hierarchy you are, but if you are someone very senior (e.g. bride or groom's mother, first speaker up on the day, etc.) then yes, it is your job to welcome everyone to the wedding and thank them for coming. Others following you will probably thank them too, but that's no bad thing. Many people will have travelled from afar, spent a lot on transport, accommodation, gift, etc., so they deserve as much gratitude as they get.

- *Welcomes the groom and his family into your own – **Yes***
  This assumes that you are speaking as a member of the bride's family. In my opinion I would say this is an essential part of your speech. Whatever you and other family members and friends may feel about the groom, this day is all about the fact that he and the bride have got married. At this time, possibly more than at any other, it's time to think, speak and be positive. No matter what you think, he is the bride's new husband and deserves a) your respect and b) your welcome. (And he may turn out to be not as bad as you thought.)

- *Thanks people for their efforts in the wedding preparations – **Yes***
  Depending on who you are you may well be one of the people who deserves thanks more than most, but even so it will be appropriate that you thank the other people responsible for making the day a success. Someone else will certainly thank you later on. And probably you shouldn't be stingy with your thanks. Even people or companies who are paid to provide services at the wedding have almost certainly put in a great deal of effort and unpaid enthusiasm which deserve a mention, at least.

- *Mention special guests who can't be present – **Yes***
  This part of the proceedings may well be allocated to another speaker, but traditionally it is the remit of the father of the bride slot and if you are performing that, then mentioning such special guests is a must. This usually covers elderly relatives and friends, relatives and friends who are indisposed for some reason, and those who are unable to travel long distances. You can also talk about deceased relatives and friends who would love to have been at the wedding, but this requires particularly delicate handling – see below.

- *Finally proposes a toast to the bride and groom – **Probably***
  This is not so much a matter of your remit in replacing the

'father of the bride' slot, as it is because you're likely to be the first speaker up on the day. The first toast is probably the most important one of all and it should be to the bride and groom.

Your structure skeleton

This is how your father of the bride speech can work out. The following would also make a sensible running order for you to use.

- **Welcome guests to the wedding**, especially if you are the first speaker of the day. Traditionally the father of the bride will have been the one who has paid for most of the wedding, so he would have been seen as the 'host' by some of the older guests at least.

- **Talk about the bride** – one or two short anecdotes about her in the past, amusing if you want but beware of making jokes here. It's far more important, in this role, to ensure that you give plenty of praise and admiration for the bride. And don't be shy about expressing your feelings towards her. Weddings are supposed to be emotional occasions. Make sure that this section of your speech, although perhaps starting with stories about the bride's childhood, ends on her encounter and relationship with the groom.

- Now **welcome the groom and his family** into your (the bride's) family, assuming you are part of the bride's family or at least a very close friend. If you don't know the groom and his family very well focus on how happy the bride is and has been since the couple met, so congratulate the groom on making her happy! You can also say how much you/the bride's family are looking forward to getting to know the groom and his people better.

- Here you can **link to absent family and friends** by saying how sad they are/would be to miss this happy day and the chance to see the bride looking so radiant. It's probably more sensible to focus on people who are alive but elsewhere. However, important recently deceased relatives can be talked about with appropriate sensitivity.

♦ You can then cheer up the mood by **thanking distant friends and relatives** who have come from afar for making the journey and making this day so special for everyone.

♦ Your next link might be to say that probably the most recognition and gratitude for making this day so special, however, must go to everyone who has put in so much time and effort on the preparations for the big day. **Name the key people** and say a few words about what each of them did.

♦ **End by saying a summarising sentence** or two about this being such a wonderful day for everyone, and our greatest thanks must go to the two people who brought us together for this event. That's your cue for words along the lines of 'and now, please raise your glasses for a toast ... ladies and gentlemen, those two fantastic people ... the bride and groom'.

VOICES OF EXPERIENCE

My sister, the bride, asked me to give the bride's father's speech, as the best solution to the perennial problem of divorced parents. The groom had already picked his sister as best man, so it fitted in perfectly. It meant all three speeches were given by members of the same generation, the only downside being that none of us would be able to speak of marriage from first-hand experience.

I avoided all but the most general and safe anecdotes. I also believe that while brides can take a little teasing from their fathers, it is not as easy to take coming from a sister – particularly as most sisters have a history of competition and mutual embarrassment. In fact, I stuck very closely to the traditional format for the bride's father, rewriting in my own idiom as much as possible.

In many ways the speech turned out to be quite serious – I didn't actually refer to the marital difficulties of our parents, but I did offer advice on the nature of love, on putting the other person first in all things and avoiding any idea that marriage was a competition, first in a comic vein, and then with more serious intent.

I was a little concerned about doing this – both bride and groom are committed Catholics, and might have thought my comments on the nature of love inappropriate. I am a practising Buddhist – and love and compassion are central to that practice. In the end, it seemed to go down very well.

I wrote the speech over the course of a week, and by the eve of the wedding had a rough draft, which I tested on the best woman (and vice versa). The rest of that day was very full, as I was also responsible for decorating the tables, and drafting seating plans, etc, so I didn't get to finish the final draft that night – I woke at 4am and finished it then! That meant I had no chance to learn it or even to print it out, so I hand-wrote it onto cards – which in itself was a kind of practice.

There wasn't any time to think about it again until after the wedding itself, at the drinks reception, by which time I was far too nervous to think about reading or practising it again.

It went very well – better than I could have hoped for. My sister was looking at me with complete terror in her eyes – but dissolved into tears halfway through at the point where I told her how amazed I was that the little scrap I used to carry about had grown into such a beautiful and poised woman. What was even better – and unscripted – was that the only other thing I had in my handbag was a huge white cotton hanky, which I handed to her to mop up. It got a round of applause.

On the whole, I felt that it had been far, far better received than I could have dreamt possible – I made them laugh, and made them cry, and I remembered to thank everyone important.

Here's my advice:

1. Stick to tradition – the rules on who thanks whom for what, and the order in which it is done are tried and tested methods, and give a rhythm to the speech – it is surprisingly easy to adapt the format to personal circumstances. You can find examples and guidelines in books, in libraries or on the internet – also read a few, and find a style or approach that you like.

2. If you are not sure whether to include someone in the list of thanks, include them – the worst it can do is make one more person happy. You don't have to share the speech in advance, but do double-check with bride and groom who you have listed in the thanks section.

3. Avoid the temptation to be mean or outrageous or obscene to get a laugh – it's really not in the spirit of the occasion – it's possible to be funny or moving, or to hold the attention without resorting to impulses which are actually pretty cruel. If you find yourself thinking 'if they don't like it they have no sense of humour' stop, and rewrite. Better to have a short, boring speech that is kind, than one people remember for being unkind or humiliating.

4. Don't drink before hand. Nothing. Not a drop. Not even a sip of champagne. You have a job to do, and you will need to be stone cold sober to do it justice. Have someone standing by with a glass as you stand to speak – your first taste should be when you propose the toast. And then you can heave a huge sigh of relief and start making up for lost time!

Anya, London

I did the father of the bride speech as my grandfather had passed away by the time my mother remarried. I bought a book on father of the bride speeches. Having read that and taking into account that I was not actually the father of the bride I put together the main points I wanted to get across then added bits to it including a few light-hearted comments as well as some serious points. I didn't practise it too much as I didn't want it to sound too rehearsed. I practised it a few times to myself and once in front of other people.

My speech seemed to go well and got laughs at the right moments! The bride and groom both liked it too (or so they say!). I felt pleased with the way it had gone but hate watching it back on the DVD! I was honoured to have done it.

My advice is:

◆ Be yourself and be natural, don't try to be something you're not.

◆ Get the basics down of what you want to say then work from there.

◆ Don't make it too long, better to be too short than send your audience to sleep.

◆ The guests will want you to do well, it's not like a business presentation or a university assessment, they will be impressed you're getting up there and doing it, relax and enjoy your moment in the limelight.

_____ *Elizabeth Lorkins*

I adhered to the traditional father of the bride speech in so far as it was possible. I welcomed everybody, especially my husband's family. I spoke about how we had organised our wedding along traditional lines, but as my father had passed away I was speaking in his place. That got applause.

I spoke about my mother's family and I acknowledged the members present and they were applauded. I acknowledged the next generation, my generation – brother, sister, first cousins etc., then moved to the next generation and acknowledged my niece and nephews who were present.

I did the same with my father's family, however, some of them had interesting names that we as children (and the adults too) did amusing things with and that got a laugh. I acknowledged the spouses and partners as appropriate.

I acknowledged all my guests and said how I met them from my first day at school, through work, courses and hobbies. I acknowledged their husbands and partners collectively.

I concluded with a toast, I asked the Irish to stand and toast the visitors. (This was appropriate as the wedding was in Ireland.)

I did not have much trouble memorising it as it was very familiar to me, but I did use cue cards in case I left anyone out. From the applause and laughter I felt it was received very well. Afterwards people complemented me on the speech.

My advice: never use risqué material. Be well prepared and confident and ensure that no one can say 'you should not have done it'.

_____ *Evelyn Khan-Panni*

IF YOU'RE SPEAKING INSTEAD OF THE BEST MAN

Here's how we can break down the elements of the traditional best man speech and see how each one should or should not be included in yours.

Content 'idea triggers'

- *Thanks the bridegroom for his speech –* **Probably**
  I only say 'probably' because you could well be thanking the bride and groom for their joint speech, rather than his alone. This is something that will (or should) be established at the planning stage.

- *(Thanks) on behalf of the bridal attendants – for his toast –* **Yes**
  This assumes that the groom or bride/groom combo have followed the traditional path and ended his/their speech by proposing a toast to the bridal attendants.

- *Talks about the groom –* **Yes**
  With all the focus on the bride that has taken place in the 'father of the bride' speech – assuming there is one – now it's the groom's turn. This is an important part of the best man's role.

- *... and his relationship with him –* **Yes, but carefully!**
  Here's where the fact that you are woman *can* make a difference, no matter how devoted their entire bridal party is to equality. A great deal depends on exactly what your relationship with the groom actually is. If you are his mother or sister you're on fairly safe ground but if you know him as a friend or ex-girlfriend, you will need to be tactful. Whether we girls like it or not, you as a woman speaker will not get away with the naughty innuendos that a male best man might. The last person you want to upset is the bride, and if there's even the faintest hint that you might be connected with any naughtiness on the groom's part in the past, she may feel slightly irritated. (Put it this way; I would!) I know that's unfair and unequal but we've just got to get over it. Wedding speeches are not the right media for breaking new ground in feminist or gender issues.

♦ *Reads out any telemessages and cards that have accumulated –* **Yes**
This is a traditional element of wedding speeches, but of course there may not be any. However it's quite likely that there will be a few cards and emails from absent friends and it can be fun to read them out. It also opens up possibilities for some light-hearted jokes (see below).

♦ *... ends by proposing a toast to the bride and groom –* **Yes**
This is particularly relevant if you are the last speaker up on the day. I know that the father of the bride speaker toasts the bride and groom as well, but it *is* their day after all!

Your structure skeleton

This is how your best man speech can work out. The following would also make a sensible running order for you to use. And don't forget, the traditional best man speech is supposed to be the most entertaining of the day. However whether you make your speech funny or not depends on you, your personality, and your style.

♦ Assuming your speech follows that of the groom or bride/groom combo, thank him/them for his/their speech and for proposing a toast to the bridal attendants. Although in theory the traditional best man role is to thank on behalf of the bridesmaids, be sure you include any ushers, pages, flower girls, etc.

♦ Now you need to link to why you're up there in the first place, by saying how you came to know the groom. If you're related to him quite a few people will know that already, but if you're a friend from elsewhere, a work colleague, etc., you should explain how you came to know each other and what great friends/ colleagues you have become.

- This is the point in the speech where the best man will usually tell some funny stories about his relationship with the groom, shared experiences, shared disasters, etc. Here you will need to think back to occasions in your relationship which are not necessarily funny but otherwise are of interest. You might recount an experience when the groom did something incredibly brave and heroic – perhaps worked through several nights to (successfully) win back an important client, climbed a dangerous rock face to raise money for charity, rescued a kitten by climbing up a tree in a high wind, entertained a group of fellow holidaymakers with magic tricks when the coach taking you all to a ski resort broke down for four hours, etc. Needless to say whatever anecdotes you recount must focus on the groom's positive qualities, and must *not* focus in any way whatsoever on sexual activities, no matter how far back in the past the stories go.

- Now bring everyone back to the present day and if there are any telegrams or emails to read out, do it. In the past it was fashionable for the best man to read out spoof telegrams that poked fun at the bride, groom and their families but that seems to be out of favour now – possibly because telegrams no longer exist *per se* and emails are very commonplace. In fact depending on how you work things out at the planning stage, if the father of the bride (or whoever is giving that introductory speech) is going to mention absent friends and family it might make more sense for him/her to read out greetings sent by the people he mentions.

- And here, it's time to wrap up, saying how proud and happy you are to see the groom marrying such a wonderful partner and wishing them every happiness in the future. Often the best man will offer some humorous advice on how to have a successful marriage but some people feel this part of the traditional speech has become something of a cliché. My own feeling is that the main advice you should give is advice that's serious and from the heart – for example if you have been happily married for many years, share your own tips. You can add in a couple of jokey lines before that if you want to, but focus on the serious – it's valuable.

◆ You could perhaps end on saying that you doubt whether the bridal couple need more than a little advice because you're certain they are destined for a wonderfully long and happy life together. Leading into something like 'and to celebrate that, ladies and gentlemen, please raise your glasses to ... [names of bride and groom].

VOICES OF EXPERIENCE

('Best man' at cousin's wedding). I acknowledged the unusualness of the situation and I spoke about the historic origins of the best man's speech. The groom introduced the theme of memory lane and I followed that theme, with my own recollections, especially of times spent with my cousin. I reminded them of woman's equality (the women loved this) and concluded with a toast to absent friends.

I practised it a lot, enough to appear off the cuff. Because I was not the traditional expected speaker there was a risk of some guests expecting a lesser performance from a woman.

It was acknowledged as the best speech of the day. I got the impression that the other speakers thought there was nothing to it. They were under prepared/ill advisedly prepared and under rehearsed. From the applause and laughter I felt it was received very well. When I mentioned that the best man was a defender in case 'a rival suitor may be lurking nearby', one of the male guests got up and closed the door. That got a laugh.

My advice: go ahead, thank the person who offered you the honour of your speaking at his/her wedding. Be confident that you are saying the right thing and don't offend anyone. Do not use any risqué material. Be well prepared and ensure that no one can say 'you should not have done it'. Be alert to possible initial resistance.

_____ *Evelyn Khan-Panni*

A very long time ago I gave a 'best woman' speech based on an anecdote of a bride and groom meeting on holiday and the groom as a renaissance man!

My advice to all women making speeches at a wedding is, forget tradition. Women have a voice and I would encourage brides, their mothers, the groom's mother and even brides-maids to get up and say what they want to say. Make it fairly short – if the speeches go on too long, guests start giving up the will to live (as in the case of my daughter and son-in-law's wedding. There were too many speeches and the Best Man went on forever – including a PowerPoint presentation of the groom growing up.)

_____ *Dawn Charles*
www.awp.ecademy.com

DOUBLE-ACT SPEECHES

At a modern wedding, two people may want to share the delivery of a speech. This can be any one of the following permutations and probably loads more:

◆ father and mother of the bride/groom
◆ best man and best woman (why shouldn't there be two?)
◆ best friends of the bridal couple
◆ sisters and/or brothers, etc.
◆ ... and of course, the bridal couple themselves.

Here are a few tips on how to ensure such double-act speeches work well.

First of all, plan your speech as carefully as you can. I know that this can be demanding, especially if the double act consists of the bride and groom, but believe me it's well worth working it through carefully. (And prior to the wedding it provides a lovely opportunity for you to disappear for an evening to 'plan your joint speech' when everyone else is running around like headless chickens.)

Really, it all comes down to dividing the material so that you don't duplicate what each other says, and that you provide an entertaining and balanced speech that shows how much both of you mean to the bridal couple – and how much they mean to you.

And above all else you must not interrupt each other, unless it's part of a pre-planned humorous exercise to tell – jointly – a joke!

The Bride – The Sky's the Limit!

You're a lucky girl in more ways than one! Not only are you the star of the day but also you have what amounts to *carte blanche* in terms of what you say in your speech – particularly if all the obligatory points have been made by the traditional male speakers. However you *will* need to decide what you're going to talk about at some point, and unless you are very good at impromptu speaking that should happen sooner rather than later.

The other thing you need to consider is that much as it's 'your day,' you need to put your speech together bearing in mind not just your own interests, but also those of the people who will hear you.

Let's have a look at areas of content you could contemplate, in no particular order.

CONTENT 'IDEA TRIGGERS'

♦ **Why we're all here**
  - This is the most wonderful day of my life.
  - I am so thrilled to see so many people I love here sharing the day with us.
  - Thank you so much for coming.
  - Thank you so much for your gifts.

♦ **Distant friends and family (present)**
  - It's especially heart warming that [people] were prepared to travel all the way from [place].
  - I'm so glad they could be here to complete our family/group of friends.
  - I have such fond memories of the great times we've had together, especially on my trips out to see them in [place].

♦ **Distant friends and family (absent)**
  - It's a great shame that [names] couldn't be here today.
  - I know they're thinking of us right now and I promised I'd have an extra drink for them. (Short anecdote about them? Joke about why they couldn't come?)

♦ **Distant friends and family (ill)**
  - It's a great shame that [name] couldn't be here today due to ill health. (Possible explanation of ill health – e.g. accident, surgery, etc.)
  - I know they're thinking of us right now and I promised I'd have an extra drink for them.
  - I'm sure you'll join me in wishing [name] a swift recovery/all the best.

♦ **Distant friends and family (deceased)**
  - I know this is hardly the time to think of sad things.
  - As you know [may not know] my [relationship], [name,] passed away [when].

- However I just wanted to say how much s/he would have enjoyed today.
- I can almost see him/her (short amusing anecdote about that person and how s/he would have reacted to this occasion?).
- I'm sure s/he is with us in spirit and s/he is very much on our minds today.

- ◆ **Appreciation of parents, parents-in-law, grandparents and grandparents-in-law**
  - Their role in your past.
  - Amusing anecdotes?
  - What they mean to you now.
  - What they have contributed to your relationship.
  - What they've contributed to this wedding.

- ◆ **Appreciation of your siblings and children**
  - Their role in your past.
  - Amusing anecdotes?
  - What they mean to you now.
  - What they have contributed to your relationship.
  - What they've contributed to this wedding.

- ◆ **Appreciation of your new family**
  - Parents-in-law.
  - Sisters and brothers-in-law.
  - Step-children.
  - Step-in-laws and siblings.
  - What they have contributed to your relationship.
  - What they've contributed to this wedding.
  - How much they will all mean to you in the future.

- ◆ **Appreciation of other members of the wedding party**
  - Your father [or whoever gives that traditional speech].
  - Your husband.
  - The best man [assuming you speak after him].

- – Your bridesmaids.
- – Pages and flower girls.
- – Other people who contributed.

♦ **Appreciation of friends**
- – Their role in your past.
- – Amusing anecdotes?
- – What they mean to you now.
- – What they have contributed to your relationship.
- – What they've contributed to this wedding.

♦ **Appreciation of colleagues**
- – Their role in your working life.
- – Amusing anecdotes?
- – What they have contributed to your relationship (if relevant).
- – What they've contributed to this wedding.
- – How your working life will be after marriage.

♦ **People to whom you might propose a toast**
- – Distant/absent friends and family.
- – Your husband.
- – Your parents.
- – Your family.
- – Your joint families.
- – Your children.
- – Your guests.

♦ **A poem, perhaps?**
- – Love poem to your husband.
- – Appreciation poem to your parents.
- – Appreciation poem to all your guests.
- – Appreciation poem to your children.

♦ **Jokes potential**
- – About yourself.
- – About your new husband.

- About your relationship/courtship/engagement.
- About marriage itself.
- About your expectations of marriage.

◆ **Other events sharing the same date**
  - Did you know that on this day in [year] [the following] happened?

YOUR STRUCTURE SKELETON

Here is a selection of raw material you can use, and the order in which you can present it, to help you create a structure for your speech. You probably won't want to use it all, but instead will retain the ideas that work for you and edit out the ideas that don't. Plus, you may want to customise it to suit your needs.

How to take it from there is described in detail in Chapter 2 – formulate a good structure and then talk it through to yourself – preferably on an audio-recording system which can then play back your 'natural' words and wording. Transcribe that, tidy it up, add a few gems like jokes, poetry, quotations if you want (see Part 3) and you've got yourself one powerful speech.

◆ Why is the bride making a speech? Many of you know I talk too much anyway, so why change the habits of a lifetime just because it's my wedding?

◆ Actually I wanted the chance to say 'thank you' to many people – in fact all of you.

◆ First I want to tell you how I met [husband] ... (short amusing, true, anecdote).

◆ Thank you so much to [(name] who introduced us.

- Thank you, too, to [name] who organised such a wonderful hen party (short amusing anecdote here).

- While I'm about it I must thank all of you for coming here today, especially those of you who have travelled from far away.

- Also I must mention [relative] who I know would have loved to be here today but sadly can't be [reason why].

- And of course I must thank you for your fabulous gifts.

- We haven't opened them yet because we're saving them for when we get back from honeymoon.

- I'd also like to thank [name, best man] for his, er, brilliant speech (perhaps quick joke here?).

- Thanks, too, to [whoever else played a particularly significant role. If you want, you can present them with gifts now].

- But perhaps more than anyone I owe thanks to, it's my parents.

- Why I owe them so much from when I was a little girl.

- Why I owe them so much now.

- How much I love them and thank them for today.

- And how much I love my work friends who have been so supportive through all my wedding plans – thanks, guys.

- And thanks, too, to my work colleagues who have been so supportive as well.

- Now, to my new husband, the most important person of all.

- My own ordinary words aren't enough to describe what I feel.

- So I will share this poem with you all. (Read poem.)

- Someone told me I should marry a rich man.

- Well, I have – a man rich in all the qualities that any woman will even need to make her happy.

- Now, a toast – to my husband, [name].

VOICES OF EXPERIENCE

I gave a speech at my own wedding five years ago. My father went first, then my husband, then me, and then the best man. All speeches were with champagne before we started eating so everyone was sober and wasn't so nervous we couldn't eat! There were over 100 guests so it was a big bash.

I wanted to give a speech because I wanted to personally thank a number of people, including my husband and both our sets of parents, and the other close friends and family who had supported me personally. It was pretty lighthearted mixed with some sentiment and heartfelt thanks. It was also much shorter than any of the other speeches. I kept it secret – I knew the rough areas the other speeches would be covering by convention and just pitched it somewhere in between. There were a couple of anecdotes about the groom and some serious stuff – mostly it was my personal acknowledgement and thanks to the special people who had helped to make the day, and our relationship, work so well.

I practised a couple of times out loud and wrote the speech out double spaced in large type on a piece of paper. I kept the speech in a folder with all my other notes and schedules for the day, which had been dropped at the venue that morning.

I was really really pleased I'd done it – although I realised too late that I had missed one person out of my thank yous, which I regretted. Somehow it made me feel much more part of the day rather than the day happening to me.

My advice is be prepared for some raised eyebrows – not everyone, including other women, thinks it's a good idea for a woman to give a wedding speech in any capacity. If you're the bride, keep it fairly short and sweet, very personal, and make sure you're not covering the same ground as the other main speeches, including cracking too many best man-style jokes. Be clear about when you will be making your speech so there isn't any miscommunication, especially if someone is announcing the speeches. Go for it!

Maja Pawinska Sims
www.be-sparkle.co.uk

I spoke last, as I stood up rather spontaneously and said I had to have the last word! It was pretty much off the cuff mainly thanking everyone for coming (particularly the Scots who had driven down to Bournemouth!) and saying things like 'you'd all given up on me ever getting married as I was 35 and on the shelf' so to speak. My brother was married at 24! Great relief from my parents etc who thought I was too much of a career girl! I made comments about Steve being my toyboy – six months younger and you're as young as the man you feel etc! How we'd get on perfectly as long as Steve did what I told him …

Julie Lacey

We didn't really have a 'traditional' wedding – we got married in St Lucia, and then had a very big party when we got back to the UK – about 400 people – my husband got stage fright and wouldn't get up and say anything. I had about one minute – whilst arguing with him behind the DJ's booth – then I just got up and said whatever came to me.

The guests were confused at first, especially as the DJ had said it was going to be my husband, but I made a joke about it and they all laughed (including him!). I didn't speak for very long (which I think they were grateful for – there was dancing to be done) and got a huge round of applause at the end and quite a few offers of marriage! The guests – they were wonderful, so kind and they obviously wanted me to do well – they wanted me to say the right things.

After the event I 'rehearsed' a lot: you know, I wish I'd said this or I wish I'd mentioned Great Auntie Edie. I still dream about it even now. My advice is be prepared and have fun – everyone wants it to go well, they don't want you to be a failure, they want you to succeed, these are mostly people that love you and care for you – they want you to be happy!

_____ *Debbie Jenkins*
www.debbiejenkins.com

We didn't have a traditional reception, particularly – we mixed the speeches in between the meal courses and music from a friend. All speeches were limited to five minutes and mine was the last one.

Mostly it was a humorous recollection of how my husband and I met. We were next-door neighbours and I did jokes about connecting doors, taxis home and footprints in the snow. I just had a flash of inspiration and wrote it down. I also used it to briefly thank various people, but not in a too gushy 'Gwyneth Paltrow at the Oscars' kind of way.

I did practise, but only really a quick run through I did have it written down word for word in a super-big font just in case I got lost.

My advice is, only do it if you really want to; not because you think you should or because it's fashionable. It wasn't fashionable when I did it (in 1998) and I'm still the only woman I know who has done so. Also only do it if you're super confident – you don't want the terror of 'the speech' ruining your big day. Write it down and practise, unless you're a master (or mistress) at speaking off the cuff. Keep it short and simple. Make it funny, if you can, but not at anyone's expense.

Helen Parkinson

The Maid/Matron of Honour/Chief Bridesmaid/Sister/Friend

If you're speaking in this role, it's possible that you may share some of the 'desirable' elements (such as giving thanks and appreciation to appropriate people) with that of a woman replacing the best man. If that's true in your case you may want to read through the section called 'If you're speaking instead of the best man' in Chapter 6 and pick up on any points in common.

More usually though your role is as a close friend/relative of the bride. Whereas in theory the best man (or best woman) is speaking as a close friend or relative of the bridegroom – that's the key difference – nowadays such traditional formalities are often disregarded. However for the sake of argument (and this chapter) let's assume you're coming in as the bride's right-hand-woman and your speech reflects this.

If there is a best man speaking as well, we will assume that he does the required thank yous and you're free to focus on sharing your fondness for the bride, anecdotes and stories about your relationship, and your delight at seeing her so happy on this day.

Let's start by looking at some areas from which you can draw ideas for speech content.

CONTENT 'IDEA TRIGGERS'

- **Why we're all here**
  - Who I am (if not properly announced).
  - Relationship to bride.
  - Here to say a few words about [bride's name].

- **If you're (happily) married**.
  - So glad [bride's name] is able to share the happiness a good marriage provides.
  - How my husband and I reacted when [bride] told us she and [groom] were getting married.

- **If you're single**
  - How envious you are of [bride's] happiness.
  - How lucky she and [groom] are.

- **If you're related to the bride**
  - How honoured you were when [bride] asked you to speak today.
  - Your earliest memories of her and your relationship.
  - Funny stories about bride as a baby/toddler/child/teenager? (not too rude!).
  - How much bride means to you and the rest of your family.

- How delighted you are to welcome [groom] into the family.
- Bride's qualities and achievements through her life (maybe five key qualities).
- How proud you all are of her today and why.

+ **If you're not related to the bride**
  - How honoured you were when [bride] asked you to speak today.
  - How you came to meet [bride].
  - What your relationship was then.
  - What you thought of each other then.
  - How your relationship has developed.
  - A couple of funny, entertaining, emotional etc. experiences you have shared.
  - Bride's qualities and achievements you admire most (maybe five key qualities).
  - Hope [groom] appreciates these qualities.

+ **The lead-up to the wedding**
  - What your involvement has been in wedding preparations.
  - What the experience has been like.
  - Any funny stories about the preparations?
  - How you and [bride] coped with stress, etc.
  - What sort of 'hen night' you organised (funny stories? Not too lurid!).

+ **The bride and groom together**
  - The first time you met [groom] and your reactions (joke?).
  - Your reaction when they announced they were getting married.
  - A few words about their children if they have any?
  - What they share in terms of love, friendship, mutual interests.
  - What if any (joke) problems they might encounter (e.g. dirty football kit!).

  – How you see their future together.

♦ **A poem, perhaps?**
  – Poem about happy marriage/happy families.
  – Funny poem about marriage (not too negative).
  – Limerick.
  – Appreciation poem to the bride.

♦ **Quotations**
  – About marriage.
  – About true love.
  – About friendship.

♦ **Jokes potential**
  – About yourself.
  – About the bride (be careful not to offend, and avoid previous boyfriends, etc!).
  – About the groom (be careful not to offend, as above).
  – About marriage itself.

♦ **Other events sharing the same date**
  – Did you know that on this day in [year] [the following] happened?

♦ **People to whom you might propose a toast:**
  – Distant/absent friends and family.
  – The bride and groom.
  – Your parents (if you're the bride's sister).
  – Your joint families – yours (if you're related to the bride) and the groom's.

YOUR STRUCTURE SKELETON

Here is a selection of raw material you can use, and the order in which you can present it, to help you create a structure for your speech. You probably won't want to use it all, but instead will retain the ideas that work for you and edit out the ideas that don't. Plus, you may want to customise it to suit your needs.

How to take it from there is described in detail in Chapter 2 – formulate a good structure and then talk it through to yourself – preferably on an audio-recording system which can then play back your 'natural' words and wording. Transcribe that, tidy it up, add a few gems like jokes, poetry, quotations if you want (see Part 3) and you've got yourself one powerful speech.

- Hello everyone and as you heard I am the [chief bridesmaid/ maid of honour/whatever].

- I am also the [bride's sister/best friend/whatever].

- When [bride] asked me to give a speech here today I was really honoured.

- (Joke perhaps, for example) I will keep it brief because of my throat [bride] threatened to slit it if I went on for more than five minutes.

- But before I go on, you may be interested to know that on today's date, [couple of examples of other great things that happened on this date in the past].

- (If you're married) As some of you know [your husband] and I have been very happily married for X years and when [bride and groom] told us they were getting married I was thrilled for them both – it really is a wonderful institution.

- (Couple of quotations or jokes perhaps, for example) A few words of advice on how to keep that marriage fresh and happy ... go out to dinner once a week. [Bride] should go on Tuesdays, [groom] should go on Thursdays.

- (If you're single) When [bride and groom] told me they were getting married of course I was delighted, but also I was a little bit envious. They are so happy together!

- (If you're related to the bride) I must tell you, though, [bride] has not always been the cool, calm, collected, mature lady she is today. When we were growing up together she was ... (think of your relationship when you were kids ... funny stories? What she did when you were little ... family holidays ... pets ... school ... teenagers ... first jobs, etc.)

- (If you're not related to the bride) I first met [bride] when we were [explanation here]. In those days she and I were [describe relationship]. In the intervening years we have been through a lot together [describe, preferably focusing on funny stories ... your social lives? Work? Holidays together?]

- But [bride] has grown into a wonderful mature woman and [groom] is so lucky to have been chosen as her husband!

- I first knew [groom] when [describe] and when he and [bride] got together, [describe your feelings ... don't be unkind! ... perhaps make a joke?].

- However as their relationship progressed we couldn't fail to see what a terrific couple they had become, and were going to be in the future.

- (If they have children) And when little [children's names] came along it just made the whole thing perfect.

- In fact, I'd like to read out this poem which expresses how we all feel, better than I can ... (Perhaps a poem here about happy families, or happy marriage.)

- You may think that just because I'm calm and relaxed now the whole lead-up to today has been easy.

- It certainly was great fun but easy isn't the word I would use to describe it. (Tell any funny stories about preparations, bride's dress, bridesmaids' dresses, hen night – but keep it clean! – shopping trips, etc.)

- Anyway, we made it to today!

- (If you've used the 'slit my throat' gag at the beginning e.g.) And before [bride] attacks my throat with that amazing sword they're going to use to cut the cake, I will stop now and propose a toast. [Give a short reason why you're toasting whoever.]

- Ladies and Gentlemen, please raise your glasses to [whoever].

VOICES OF EXPERIENCE

From memory, there were the traditional male speeches, but my friend, being my friend, she wasn't going to leave herself out from making her speech and I remember thinking 'Good for you' and that's something I could do when my turn comes (it hasn't yet!). I guess my mind must've wandered off at some point because before I knew it, my friend announced that she wanted all the people who helped her and her new husband to get to the registry office on time to stand up, get the applause, haul themselves up to the wedding table and say a few words...

I've got a reasonably good memory, so most of the speech material – done off the cuff which is hard at the best of times and not done unless you've really got confidence – was literally from that computer called my brains and the speech was done there and then. However, I did have to be very careful over what I said and how I said it as in the run-up to their wedding, there was so much tension and friction, I was afraid they wouldn't get married, never mind me having a captive audience to deliver my speech to!

I'm afraid there was no practice and precious little rehearsal but as I had known the couple for several years, the best I can say is that there was an intuitive trust that I would say the right thing on the grounds of being a writer!

What advice would I give? Don't be drunk when you give your speech (unforgivable!), have a small crib card for the important points if needed, keep it short, and sweet and if you really want to tell that risqué story about the couple, check with them first before you tell it!

_____*Caroline Lashley, The Editor's Office*
www.theeditorsoffice.co.uk

My friend *(the bride)* politely told me I was too old to be a bridesmaid so I joked about being best woman! Her father wouldn't let me off the hook once I'd said it as a passing joke.

My speech preceded the best man's. I sat at the top table on the insistence of my friend's father.

Initially it was a speech followed by a poem. The content focused on my friend's inability to make decisions with particular reference to the time it took to decide to date her husband and finally marry him. This led on to how her indecisive nature impacted on the stress levels of her three closest friends when they accompanied her on the wedding dress hunt. I followed it with a poem about our friendship and its value to us all. It was a mixture of laughter and tears.

I wrote the speech and the poem over the weeks leading up to the big day and rehearsed it every day. When we arrived at the hotel for the reception I decided it wasn't good enough and threw everything away. Within the time available before the wedding breakfast I concocted a new speech and decided to write a poem as well. The whole speech/poem lasted about 10 minutes. I amazed myself that under pressure and by relating true stories my final effort was the best! I became quite choked as I was speaking and I was very emotional.

Everyone laughed in the right places and cried in the right places and applauded when I finished. The guests were very kind and encouraging. Many came to me afterwards to say how much they had enjoyed it. Several female guests said how much it reminded them of their own friendships. I guess girls are just girls wherever and whoever we are!

Afterwards I was on a high, especially when the toastmaster asked if I gave wedding speeches for a job! I felt good because my friend loved it and I know it contributed to her day. I felt bad because the best man's speech was an anticlimax afterwards.

My advice to other women is, speak from the heart and with sincerity. You are doing this for someone you love and care for. Generally the truth is funnier and better received than joke telling. Don't throw banana skins in front of yourself – i.e. don't say anything that could cause you to fall flat! Use notes if you need to. Remember the guests/audience are rooting for you. There is no way most of them would be up there themselves!

Christine Knott
www.beyondthebox.co.uk

Mother, Grandmother, or Other Older Relative of Bride or Groom

Mothers and other older female relatives are in an envious position when speeches are called for, if only because you can get away with being funny, romantic, sentimental or even downright soppy. That's because you're either 'Mum' or someone similar and we ladies of a certain age – especially when closely connected with such an emotionally charged event – are expected to let the whole wedding thing render us incapable of rational thought.

The fact that many mothers of the bride or groom or even grandmothers of the bride or groom are not only doting mumsies but also chief executives, entrepreneurs, politicians, charity fund-raisers, or any one of hundreds of other such unsoppy activities, escapes most wedding audiences entirely.

And that issue is not exclusive to the audience, either. It will also get to you. Even if you feel perfectly comfortable addressing a few hundred company shareholders or employees at a business conference, don't think you'll be able to hide behind your corporate persona when you speak at the wedding of your daughter/son/niece/nephew/godchild/grandchild/stepchild etc. You won't, because you'll be there as yourself, not the boss/CEO/chairperson.

However, don't let that worry you. Unlike what's required for a business conference or fund-raising meeting, all you need for this speech to be a great success is to be yourself and talk about what really matters to you personally.

KEEP IT SHORT

Although no one would be so rude as to tell you to keep your speech short, the reality is it should be. Much as we Mums play what no one can deny is a pretty important role in getting the bride or groom to the altar in the first place, when it comes to the wedding speeches we are *not* one of the front runners. Unless your speech is actually replacing one of the key mainstays – i.e. the traditional father of the bride or best man roles – it shouldn't be as long as the main speeches.

Also – despite what I said about being able to get away with being anything from funny to soppy – you won't get away with it if it takes longer than about five minutes.

So, let's move on and look at some areas from which you can draw ideas for speech content.

CONTENT 'IDEA TRIGGERS'

◆ **Why we're all here**
   - Who I am (if not properly announced).
   - Relationship to bride/groom.
   - Here to say a few words about [bride's/groom's name].

◆ **If you're (happily) married**
   - So glad [bride's/groom's name] able to share the happiness a good marriage provides.
   - How my husband and I reacted when [bride/groom] told us s/he and [bride/groom] were getting married.

◆ **If you're single (and not a parent/grandparent)**
   - How envious you are of [bride's/groom's] happiness.
   - How lucky s/he and [bride/groom] are.

◆ **The background**
   - How honoured you were when [bride/groom] asked you to speak today.
   - Your earliest memories of him/her and your relationship.
   - Funny stories about [bride/groom] as a baby/toddler/child/teenager? (not too rude or embarrassing!).
   - How much [bride/groom] means to you and the rest of your family.
   - [Bride's/groom's] qualities and achievements through her/his life (maybe five key qualities).
   - How proud you all are of her/him today and why.

◆ **Family issues**
   - How pleased you are that [bride/groom] is marrying into the [name] family.
   - Your relationship with that family. (Known them for a long time? What stories are there to tell about that friendship? Only met them recently? Any amusing stories related to that?)

◆ **The lead-up to the wedding**
  – What your involvement has been in wedding preparations.
  – What the experience has been like. (Any funny stories about the preparations?)
  – How you and [bride/groom] coped with stress, etc.
  – How you and other older relatives/friends viewed the run-up to the wedding.
  – How this reminded you/your husband/partner of your own wedding?

◆ **The bride and groom together**
  – The first time you met [bride/groom] and your reactions (joke?)
  – Your reaction when they announced they were getting married.
  – A few words about their children if they have any?
  – What they share in terms of love, friendship, mutual interests.
  – What if any (joke) problems they might encounter (e.g. dirty football kit!).
  – How you see their future together.
  – Some sage advice from an older woman (funny?).

◆ **A poem, perhaps?**
  – Poem about happy marriage/happy families.
  – Funny poem about marriage (not too negative).
  – Limerick.
  – Appreciation poem to the [bride/groom/both].

◆ **Quotations**
  – About marriage.
  – About true love.
  – About friendship.

◆ **Jokes potential**
  – About yourself.

- – About the bride (be careful not to offend, and avoid previous boyfriends, etc!).
- – About the groom (be careful not to offend, as above).
- – About marriage itself.

◆ **Other events sharing the same date**
- – Did you know that on this day in [year] [the following] happened?

◆ **People to whom you might propose a toast**
- – Distant/absent/deceased friends and family.
- – The bride and groom.
- – Your joint families.

YOUR STRUCTURE SKELETON

Here is a selection of raw material you can use, and the order in which you can present it, to help you create a structure for your speech. You probably won't want to use it all, but instead will retain the ideas that work for you and edit out the ideas that don't. Plus, you may want to customise it to suit your needs.

How to take it from there is described in detail in Chapter 2 – formulate a good structure and then talk it through to yourself – preferably on an audio-recording system which can then play back your 'natural' words and wording. Transcribe that, tidy it up, add a few gems like jokes, poetry, quotations if you want (see Part 3) and you've got yourself one powerful speech.

◆ Hello everyone and as you heard I am [relationship to bride/ groom].

◆ I'm so happy to be here, and to be speaking at this event.

◆ All I have to do is look around to see how right this union is.

- I'm impressed by the love and friendship that is evident everywhere.

- At my age I've been to quite a few weddings.

- I always find them emotional occasions.

- (Mention earlier weddings in your family? Funny stories?)

- So if I get a bit emotional you'll have to forgive me.

- I know I'm not alone in this, either.

- In fact before we go any further I'd like to salute all the other 'older' relatives.

- Because we've been through the highs and lows of life we have a lot of experience.

- And for the same reasons, we older people are even more full of joy today.

- This would seem the right time to thank a few people.

- For example, my daughter/son's new family-in-law.

- Tribute to them.

- We (in our family) look forward to getting to know them better and sharing life's family ups and downs. (Funny stories about 'down' issues in your family jokes, perhaps?)

- And (if the bridal couple have children) I want to say a few words about my joy of being a grandparent/great-aunt, etc.

- I'm so thrilled that our extended family has become even more close as a result of today.

- However, I'm also aware that older family members like me need to step back.

- Much as we want to help, love and cherish.

- The young marrieds need to get on with their own lives.

- I will try *so* hard to avoid interfering (mother-in-law joke here?)

- However, before I stop interfering I want to say thank you to [opposite family] for the introduction of their wonderful [daughter/son] into our family.

- I can tell from the look on my [daughter/son/nephew/etc's] face that today's event is the most wonderful thing ever to happen to [him/her].

- And now I turn to my [daughter/son/niece/nephew/etc him/ herself].

- This is where I could burst into tears, so if I do please bear with me if I do.

- Also please forgive me for being sentimental but I really do love you very much.

- And I'm not the only one in this room to feel that way – not by a long way.

- Let me take 30 seconds or so to tell you why [bride/groom's name] has always been so special.

- When s/he was a little baby (stories, jokes, etc.).

- When s/he was a toddler (stories, jokes, etc.).

- When s/he was in primary school (stories, jokes, etc.).

- When s/he was going through puberty (stories, jokes, etc.).

- When s/he was a teenager (stories, jokes, etc.).

- When s/he was in their 20s (stories, jokes, etc.).

- Now – as an adult – I see how you have evolved into someone to sustain a successful marriage.

- Now – as an older [having been through one or more marriages already] adult – how I see that you have evolved into someone to sustain a successful relationship.

- In the final analysis we're all here to celebrate.

- May I reiterate how thrilled I am to be celebrating this event with my [son/daughter/whoever].

- And may I now ask you to be upstanding and toast ... Ladies and Gentlemen, the [bride and groom, or whoever you feel inclined to toast].

THE VOICE OF EXPERIENCE

As aunt of the bridegroom, I told stories about my nephew as a child and his determination, I used their joint love of (and talent for) music as a theme, used a poem (forgotten which) and a joke about them meeting. I also found out that the Beatles *All You Need is Love* became a number one hit on the same day as their wedding.

My role at my daughter's wedding was slightly more formal – I was asked to toast absent friends. I read out a number of letters and messages, most from my family in America who couldn't come. My sister got her primary school class of 8-year-olds to write their advice to the couple on how to have a happy marriage and I read some of the more hilarious excerpts. I also introduced an American tradition to the wedding, of clinking glasses with spoons to get the bride and groom to kiss. And I cried.

My advice is, forget tradition! Women have a voice and I would encourage brides, their mothers, the groom's mother and even bridesmaid to get up and say what they want to say. Make it fairly short – if the speeches go on too long, guests start giving up the will to live (as in the case of my daughter and son-in-law's wedding. There were too many speeches and the Best Man went on forever – including a PowerPoint presentation of the groom growing up.)

_____ *Dawn Charles*
www.awp.ecademy.com

The Bride or Bridegroom's Daughter

If you're speaking in this role, it's probable that this is a subsequent marriage for your parent at least, if not for both bride and groom. As you have been asked or have asked to speak at the wedding we can assume that there are few if any political issues regarding your parent's new marriage and his/her new spouse. However whether we like it or not there is bound to be some 'history'.

Here more than in any other circumstances, probably, you need to be very careful not to step on painful corns. No matter how civilised and adult everyone is within extended and step-families, there still will be sensitivities and this is one occasion when it really is unforgivable to mention anything that jars. Like I said earlier in this book, never forget whose wedding it is. It's their day and no one has the right to spoil it, even by accident.

So what's the answer? Our good old, loyal friend, positive thinking. Focus on all the positive aspects of your parent and your relationship with him/her. Even if your relationship with his/her new spouse isn't all it could be, there are still positive things you can look at in him/her. (S/he obviously makes your parent happy, for starters.)

There are many variables here depending on how old you are, how old your parent and his/her new spouse are, and what the background is to the new marriage. As with speeches in any other role you'll need to develop your speech content with these circumstances in mind. Let's start by looking at some areas from which you can draw ideas for speech content.

CONTENT 'IDEA TRIGGERS'

- ◆ **Why we're all here**
  - – Who I am (if not properly announced).
  - – Daughter (niece, god-daughter perhaps?).
  - – Here to say a few words about [my mother/father/the bridal couple].
  - – Speaking on behalf of the [XXX] family?

- ◆ **Your parent and your relationship with him/her**
  - – How honoured you were when [parent] asked you to speak today.
  - – Your earliest memories of him/her and your relationship.
  - – Funny stories about him/her from when you were a [baby/toddler/child/teenager] (not too rude!).
  - – How much s/he means to you and the rest of your family.
  - – Your parent's qualities and achievements through his/her life (maybe five key qualities).
  - – How proud you all are of him/her today and why.

- **Your new step-parent and your relationship with him/her**
  - How delighted you are to welcome [new spouse] into our family.
  - How we reacted when [parent] told us s/he and [spouse] were getting married.
  - How any grandchildren reacted.
  - How you came to meet [spouse].
  - What your relationship was then.
  - What you thought of each other then.
  - How your relationship has developed.
  - A couple of funny, entertaining, emotional etc. experiences you have shared.
  - [Spouse's] qualities and achievements you admire most (maybe five key qualities).
  - Hope [parent] appreciates those.
  - How pleased we were to meet [spouse's family].
  - How we're looking forward to getting to know them better.
  - What [parent and spouse] share in terms of love, friendship, mutual interests.
  - What if any [joke] problems they might encounter (e.g. huge extended family, expensive at Christmas/Hannukah/etc).
  - How you see their future together.

- **The lead up to the wedding**
  - What your involvement has been in wedding preparations.
  - What the experience has been like. Any funny stories about the preparations?
  - How you and (parent) coped with stress, etc.
  - What sort of 'hen night' you organised (if bride is your mother!) (funny stories? Not too lurid).

- **A poem, perhaps?**
  - Poem about happy marriage/happy families.
  - Funny poem about marriage (not too negative).

    – Limerick.
    – Appreciation poem to your parent.
    – Appreciation poem to your parent and new spouse.

◆ **Quotations**
    – About marriage.
    – About true love.
    – About friendship.

◆ **Jokes potential**
    – About yourself.
    – About parent (be careful not to offend, and avoid sensitive issues, previous history, etc!).
    – About the new spouse (be very careful not to offend, as above).
    – About marriage itself.

◆ **Other events sharing the same date**
    – Did you know that on this day in [year] [the following] happened?

◆ **People to whom you might propose a toast:**
    – Distant/absent friends and family.
    – The bride and groom.
    – Your joint families – yours and the new spouse's.

YOUR STRUCTURE SKELETON

Here is a selection of raw material you can use, and the order in which you can present it, to help you create a structure for your speech. You probably won't want to use it all, but instead will retain the ideas that work for you and edit out the ideas that don't. Plus, you may want to customise it to suit your needs.

How to take it from there is described in detail in Chapter 2 – formulate a good structure and then talk it through to yourself – preferably on an audio-recording system which can then play back your 'natural' words and wording. Transcribe that, tidy it up, add a few gems like jokes, poetry, quotations if you want (see Part 3) and you've got yourself one powerful speech.

- Hello everyone and as you heard I am [parent's] daughter.

- I'm so happy to be here, and to be speaking at this event.

- In fact I say that on behalf of the whole [parent's] family.

- I was thrilled when [Mum/Dad] asked me to say a few words today.

- (If you're married, perhaps make joke about how s/he wanted some advice about marriage.)

- Wasn't always that way around.

- When I was little, s/he taught me so much.

- (Anecdotes from your childhood?)

- (A poem about parent/child relationship?)

- I grew up to admire [parent] for [qualities].

- A wonderful person and now s/he has found a wonderful partnership.

- We were all so delighted when [parent] met [spouse].

- (Funny story or joke about when they first met?)

- My children took to [him/her] immediately.

- I was thrilled to have a new babysitter.

- It took a while to get to know each other well.

- We really appreciate how happy [s/he] makes my [parent].

- [S/he] is (key qualities).

- [Mum/Dad], I hope you appreciate these things.

- We've really enjoyed meeting [spouse's] family.

- Wondering if we should build an extension to our dining room as we'll now be at least [XX] for family dinners.

- But what fun we will have.

- And at the heart of it this wonderful relationship between [Mum/Dad] and [spouse].

- Mind you, I'm surprised [spouse] is still even talking to [Mum/Dad] after the party we gave for [Mum/Dad's] [stag/hen/night]. (Funny stories about that?)

- And things got a little stressed when (funny story about wedding preparations?)

- But everything was OK in the end.

- [Mum/Dad] and [spouse], I can't say just how happy we are for you today.

- In fact it's better expressed by this short poem by [poet] that I/ [whoever] wrote. (Read poem.)

- Thank you both for sharing this day with us all.

- (If you're not toasting them) But I would also like to pay tribute to [whoever].

◆ (Why you want to pay tribute to them.)

◆ And may I now ask you to be upstanding and toast ... Ladies and Gentlemen, the [bride and groom, or whoever you're toasting].

Part 3

Content Resources

Jokes – Some Samples and How to Use Them

JOKES ... THE BIG ISSUE

In Chapter 3 I tried to share with you the basics of expressing humour in speeches, and I hope that has made sense to you. In this chapter though, where we're talking resources and actual jokes rather than theory, I've had to rely on my own taste and judgement by selecting jokes – or at least joke bases – that I think would work well for you.

Out there on the internet (see Resources, pages 204–5) there are thousands of jokes about weddings, marriage, love, men, women and a zillion other topics. But the trouble is, so many of them are negative and not very funny. What I've tried to do here is assemble some sample jokes that are a) appropriate for women to recount, as most wedding jokes are intended to be spoken by men and b) funny without being overly negative or bitchy about the whole marriage thing.

Obviously if you want to go for jokes and gags that do send up marriage and all that surrounds it, you have many options to choose from and I have indicated where to find those in Resources, pages 204–5.

However, well ... maybe I'm a bit of a romantic and all that, but I think women can make jokes that are a cut above the run-of-the-mill sarcastic, wee-wee taking gags you'll find in the majority of wedding speech books and on wedding websites. A little irony is great, but too much – frankly – sucks. (You'll find my email details elsewhere in this book if you want to share your disagreement with me!)

Some mechanical details

Throughout this chapter you'll find short sections in *italics* and some using capital letters in (BRACKETS).

The sections in italics are my suggestions for how you could personalise some or all of the joke in your speech. You will obviously want to adapt that to your own style and circumstances. But don't forget to do it. That way the audience won't know until a little later that you're *not* saying something seriously – which makes the joke funnier.

The capitals in brackets are intended as 'stage directions' to help you make the joke work.

I hope you have as many laughs reading – and using – these jokes as I had when putting them together!

MEN

I'm delighted to say that [bride] has given a really useful gift to (groom) as a wedding present. It's a two-day course that would benefit any typical man. *(PULL OUT A PIECE OF PAPER AND READ FROM IT – SELECT AND WRITE IN YOUR FAVOURITES FROM THE LIST BELOW!)* Here are some of the topics they'll be learning:

How to fill ice cube trays.
Step-by-step guide with slide presentation.

Toilet rolls – do they grow on holders?
Roundtable discussion.

Differences between dirty washing basket and the floor.
Practising with hamper, includes pictures and graphics.

Crockery and cutlery: do they fly to the kitchen sink or dishwasher by themselves?
Debate among a panel of experts.

Learning how to find things.
Open forum entitled, 'Starting with looking in the right place instead of turning the house upside down while screaming'.

Empty milk cartons: do they belong in the fridge or in the rubbish bin?
Group discussion and role play.

Health watch: bringing her flowers is not harmful to your health.
PowerPoint presentation.

Real men ask for directions when they're lost.
Real life testimonial from the one man who did.

Is it genetically impossible to sit quietly while she parallel parks the car?
Driving simulation.

How to be the ideal shopping companion.
Relaxation exercises, meditation and breathing techniques.

Remember important dates and telephoning when you're going to be late.
Bring your diary or PDA to class.

Now, we all know just how much careful planning and preparation has gone into this wonderful day and I really do congratulate [woman's name] on organising everything so beautifully. But can you imagine how things would have been if organising the wedding had been left up to the men?

(YOU MAY BE ABLE TO PERSONALISE THE FOLLOWING, ESPECIALLY IF YOU KNOW THE GROOM AND/OR BEST MAN HAS FAVOURITE BRANDS OF BEER, TYPES OF FOOD, ETC.)

The bride's dress would show cleavage, her navel and be tightly fitted around her bottom.

Bridesmaids would wear matching denim micro skirts and skimpy halter tops.

Morning suits/dress suits would have team logos on the back and the Nike shoes would have matching team colours.

Summer weddings would be planned around the soccer Cup Finals and county cricket.

Idiots that tried to dance with the bride would get punched in the head, unless they were really old.

Instead of a sit-down dinner or a buffet, there would be a hog roast, a barbecue, or a special order from McDonalds, KFC, or the Balti Curry House up the road.

Drinks would consist of copious quantities of Foster's with a few Bacardi Breezers for the girls.

The bridal bouquet could be recycled from a previous funeral or something.

MEN AND WOMEN

A man will pay £20 for a £10 item he needs.
A woman will pay £10 for a £20 item that she doesn't need.

A woman worries about the future until she gets a husband.
A man never worries about the future until he gets a wife.

A successful man is one who makes more money than his wife can spend.
A successful woman is one who can find such a man.

To be happy with a man, you must understand him a
lot and love him a little.
To be happy with a woman, you must love her a lot
and not try to understand her at all.

(THIS IS A LONG ONE BUT IS ESPECIALLY APPROPRIATE IF THE
BRIDE AND GROOM WORK TOGETHER, OR PLAN TO.) *These
days no one bats an eyelid when husband and wife work
together as [bride and groom] do. In fact it's usually a
highly effective partnership. But it hasn't always been that
way. Take, for example, this couple from* (NAME A CITY
REASONABLY LOCAL TO THE WEDDING) *back in the 1960s.*

On their wedding night, the bride approached her new
husband and asked for £10 for their first lovemaking
encounter. In his highly aroused state, her husband
readily agreed.

This scenario was repeated each time they made love, for
more than 30 years, with him thinking that it was a cute
way for her to afford new clothes and other incidentals
that she needed.

Arriving home around lunchtime one day, she was
surprised to find her husband very drunk. He explained
that his employer was going through a process of
corporate downsizing, and he had been made redundant.
It was unlikely that, at the age of 59, he'd be able to
find another job that paid anywhere near what he'd been
earning, and therefore, they were financially ruined.

Calmly, his wife handed him bank statements which showed more than thirty years of steady deposits and interest totalling nearly £1 million. Then she showed him certificates of deposits issued by the bank which were worth over £2 million, and told him that they had the most substantial savings that branch of the bank had ever known. She explained that while she was charging him for making love all these years, she had invested every penny and they were now millionaires.

Her husband was so astounded he could barely speak, but finally he found his voice and blurted out, 'If I'd had any idea what you were doing, I would have given you all my business!'

Well, some men just don't know when to shut up, because that's when she shot him.

———————————————

(THIS ONE MIGHT BE APPROPRIATE IF YOUR SPEECH IS REPLACING THAT OF A BEST MAN.) *I really feel that in my role as best man today I ought to tell a joke or two, in that tradition. However being a woman, I'd like to share this particular story with you … it's a girls' story but I hope all the men here who have a sense of humour will enjoy it as much as we do.*

A woman was sitting at a bar enjoying an after work cocktail with her girlfriends when an exceptionally tall, handsome, extremely sexy middle-aged man entered. He was so striking that the woman could not take her eyes off him. The young-at-heart man noticed her overly attentive stare and walked directly toward her (as all men will). Before she could offer her apologies for so rudely staring, he leaned over and whispered to her, 'I'll do anything, absolutely anything, that you want me to do, no matter how kinky, for £20 ... on one condition'. (There are always conditions.) Flabbergasted, the woman asked what the condition was. The man replied, 'You have to tell me what you want me to do in just three words.' (Controlling, huh?) The woman considered his proposition for a moment, then slowly removed a £20 bill from her purse, which she pressed into the man's hand along with her address. She looked deeply into his eyes, and slowly, and meaningfully said ...

'Clean my house.'

(THIS MIGHT BE A GOOD ICE-BREAKER AT THE BEGINNING OF YOUR SPEECH.) *I thought the service today was absolutely delightful and the prayers, especially, I found incredibly moving. It did occur to me to suggest a couple of other prayers to be spoken by [bride] and [groom], but sadly the others talked me out of it. All the same I thought you'd like to hear what I had in mind ...*

[Bride's] Prayer
Before I lay me down to sleep,
I pray for a man, who's not a creep,
One who's handsome, smart and strong,
One who loves to listen long,
One who thinks before he speaks,

One who'll call, not wait for weeks.
I pray he's gainfully employed,
When I spend his cash, won't be annoyed.
Pulls out my chair and opens my door,
Massages my back and begs to do more.
Oh! Send me a man who'll make love to my mind,
Knows what to answer to 'how big's my behind?'
I pray that this man will love me to no end,
And always be my very best friend.
Amen.

[Groom's] Prayer

I pray for a deaf-mute nymphomaniac with big boobs who owns an off-licence shop and a boat. This doesn't rhyme and I don't give a toss.

MARRIAGE

(THIS COULD FOLLOW A SECTION IN WHICH YOU TALK ABOUT WHEN THE GROOM PROPOSED TO THE BRIDE.) *Mind you, it was just as well that [groom] popped the question so directly to [bride] and there were no misunderstandings. Not like Bill and Lynn, some friends of mine from [place of your choice].*

For months Bill had been Lynn's devoted admirer. Now, at long last, he had gathered enough courage to ask her the most momentous of all questions. 'There are quite a lot of advantages to being a bachelor,' Bill began, 'but there comes a time when one longs for the companionship of another being, a being who will regard one as perfect, as an idol; whom one can treat as one's absolute own; who will be kind and faithful when times are hard; who will share one's joys and sorrows.'

To his delight, Bill saw a sympathetic gleam in Lynn's eyes. Then she nodded in agreement. Finally, Lynn responded, 'I think it's a great idea! Can I help you choose your puppy?'

Well, speaking as a happily married woman I have to give [bride and groom] some useful advice.

For starters, you must go out to dinner twice a week. *[Groom] should go on Tuesdays, [bride] on Thursdays.*

It's also a good idea to sleep in separate beds – *[groom's] in London, [bride's] in Birmingham.*

Some advice for [groom] the best time to do the washing-up is right after [bride] tells you to.

These are the three true options to consider when married people say they've never argued in more than 40 years of marriage...

1. They're lying.
2. They have very poor memories.

3. Or, they've led a very, very, dull life together.

(FIND OUT IF THE BRIDE INTENDS TO USE HER HUSBAND'S NAME, KEEP HER OWN, OR COMBINE THE TWO NAMES.) *As you may already know [bride and groom] intend to [whatever option they're going to use]. But it doesn't always work out quite so well. For example:*

If Yoko Ono had married Sonny Bono, she'd have been Yoko Ono Bono.

If Dolly Parton had married Salvador Dali, she'd be Dolly Dali.

If Olivia Newton-John married Wayne Newton, then divorced him to marry Elton John, she'd be Olivia Newton-John Newton John.

If Sondra Locke married Elliott Ness, then divorced him to marry Herman Munster, she'd become Sondra Locke Ness Munster.

If Bea Arthur married Sting, she'd be Bea Sting.

If the rap singer Snoop Dogg married Winnie the Pooh, he'd be Snoop Dogg Pooh.

If Woody Allen had married Natalie Wood, divorced her and married Gregory Peck, divorced him and married Ben Hur, he'd be Woody Wood Peck Hur.

If Dolly Parton married Tommy Smothers, then went even further back in show business and married Mr Lucky, then divorced and married Martin Short, then divorced and married American football player Ray Guy, we could all nod understandingly when we heard, 'Dolly Parton Smothers Lucky Short Guy.'

Here's a tip for [groom] on how to be the perfect husband always remember [bride's] birthday and always forget her age!

WEDDINGS

You know, when I was single I would go to family weddings and old aunts would come up to me, poke me in the ribs and cackle, saying, 'you're next'. They stopped when I started doing the same thing to them at funerals.

D'you know, I think [groom] and [bride's father] have a lot in common. Interestingly many girls seem to marry guys who are like their fathers. Perhaps that's why you see so many Mums crying at weddings.

NEWLY-WEDS

Of course we all know that [bride and groom] have a very equal and well balanced relationship, but if ever there's any doubt we should learn from this young couple who were in their honeymoon suite on their wedding night. As she got undressed for bed, her husband threw his trousers across to her and said, 'Here, put these on.' She put them on and of course they were way too big for her.

'I can't wear your trousers,' she said.

'Right,' said the husband, 'and don't you ever forget it. I'm the man who wears the trousers in this family!'

With that, she chucked her knickers over to him and said, 'put these on.' He tried, but of course he could only get them on as far as his knee.

He said, 'Damn, I can't get into your knickers!'

And she said, 'That's right – and that's how it's going to stay until you stop being such a male chauvinist pig.'

One thing about living together and getting married is that it can take some of the romance away from a relationship. For example, (GIVE A GENTLE EXAMPLE OF EITHER BRIDE OR GROOM'S PERSONAL 'HABITS' THAT THEY MIGHT NOT OTHERWISE REVEAL!) *But that's nothing compared to a couple from [name city] I heard about recently.*

They had decided to get married and as the big day approached, they grew apprehensive. Each had a problem they had never before shared with anyone, not even each other. The groom-to-be, hoping to overcome his fear, decided to ask his father for advice. 'Father,' he said, 'I am deeply concerned about the success of my marriage.'

His father replied, 'Do you love this girl?'

'Oh yes, very much,' he said,' but you see, I have very smelly feet, and I'm afraid that my fiancée will be put off by them.'

'No problem,' said dad, 'all you have to do is wash your feet as often as possible, and always wear socks, even to bed.'

Well, to him this seemed a workable solution.

The bride-to-be, overcoming her fear, decided to discuss her problem with her mom. 'Mom,' she said, 'When I wake up in the morning my breath is truly awful.'

'Don't worry, love,' her mother consoled, 'everyone has bad breath in the morning.'

'No, you don't understand. My morning breath is so bad, I'm afraid that my fiancé will not want to sleep in the same room with me.'

Her mother said simply, 'In the morning, get straight out of bed, and head for the kitchen and make breakfast. While the family is busy eating, go to the bathroom and brush your teeth. The key is, not to say a word until you've brushed your teeth.'

'I shouldn't say good morning or anything?' the daughter asked.

'Not a word,' her mother affirmed.

'Well, it's certainly worth a try,' she thought.

The loving couple were finally married. Not forgetting the advice each had received, he with his perpetual socks and she with her morning silence, they managed quite well. That is, until about six months later. Shortly before dawn one morning, the husband wakes with a start to find that one of his socks had come off. Fearful of the consequences, he frantically searches the bed. This, of course, wakes his bride and without thinking, she asks, 'What on earth are you doing?'

'Oh, my God,' he replies, 'you've swallowed my sock!'

MAKING SPEECHES

(AT BEGINNING OF YOUR SPEECH) Speech-making is a bit like prospecting for black gold. If you don't strike oil in 10 minutes, stop boring. So I'd better get on with this one!

(AT THE BEGINNING OF YOUR SPEECH) I'm told that the best speech-makers follow three simple rules. Stand up. Speak up. Then, very quickly, shut up. I'll try to stick to that advice.

Before I finish, let me just remind you of something that Lord Mancroft once said ... a speech is like a love affair. Any fool can start it, but to end it requires considerable skill. *Well, I can think of no more skilful and delightful way to end this speech, than by asking you please to stand up and raise your glasses to ...*

I know some people think it's a bit of novelty that a woman should be making a speech at a wedding. But if there is anyone here thinks it's easy compared with making the best man's speech, let me remind you about Fred Astaire and Ginger Rogers. They were probably the most successful dance partnership ever. Fred Astaire of course, was a superb dancer. But so was Ginger Rogers. And she had to do it all going backwards in high heels.

Making a speech like this is a bit like having children – easy to conceive, but hard to deliver.

FATHERS

(THIS ONE COULD BE TOLD BY THE BRIDE, THE SISTER OR MOTHER OF THE BRIDE, OR THE GROOM'S DAUGHTER. I'VE DONE A SAMPLE LEAD-IN WHICH YOU SHOULD BE ABLE TO ADAPT. WHEN THE TIME COMES PULL OUT A PIECE OF PAPER AND READ FROM IT. MAKE YOUR SELECTION FROM THE FOLLOWING.)

The other day I was clearing out some old papers and I found this – some rules that Dad had written out when I/ [bride] was pretty young but starting to go out with boys.

Rule One. If you pull your car into my drive and hoot your horn you'd better be delivering a parcel, because I can promise you you're not picking anything up.

Rule Two. You do not touch my daughter in front of me. You may glance at her, so long as you do not peer at anything below her neck. If you cannot keep your eyes or hands off my daughter's body, I will remove them. Probably with my ceremonial sword.

Rule Three. I'm sure you've been told that in today's world, sex without utilising a 'barrier method' of some kind can kill you. Let me elaborate. When it comes to sex, I am the barrier. And I certainly *will* kill you.

Rule Four. It is usually understood that in order for us to get to know each other, we should talk about sports, politics, and other issues of the day. Please do not do this. The only information I require from you is an indication of when you expect to have my daughter safely back at my house, and the only word I need from you on this subject is 'early'.

Rule Five. I have no doubt you are a popular fellow, with many opportunities to go out with other girls. This is fine with me as long as it is okay with my daughter. Otherwise, once you have gone out with my little girl, you will continue to go out with no one but her until she is finished with you. If you make her cry, I will make you cry.

Rule Six. As you stand in my front hall waiting for my daughter to appear, and more than an hour goes by, do not sigh and fidget. If you want to be on time for the cinema, you should not be going out with a girl. My daughter is putting on her make-up, a process that can take longer than painting the Forth Road Bridge. Instead of just standing there, why don't you do something useful, like changing the oil in my car?

Rule Seven. The following places are not appropriate for a date with my daughter. Places where there are beds, sofas, or anything softer than a wooden stool. Places where there are no parents, policemen, or nuns within eyesight. Places where there is darkness. Places where there is dancing or holding hands. Places where the ambient temperature is warm enough to induce my daughter to wear shorts, tank tops, midriff T-shirts, or anything other than overalls, a sweater, and a heavy anorak zipped up to her throat. Films with a strong romantic or sexual theme are to be avoided; films which feature chain saws are okay. Soccer matches are okay. Senior citizens' homes are better.

Rule Eight. Do not lie to me. On issues relating to my daughter, I am the all-knowing, merciless god of your universe. If I ask you where you are going and with whom, you have one chance to tell me the truth, the whole truth and nothing but the truth. I have a shotgun, a spade, and five acres of deserted wasteland just behind the house. Do not trifle with me.

Rule Nine. Be afraid. Be very afraid. It takes very little for me to mistake the sound of your car in the drive for a chopper coming in over a muddy field near Goose Green. When my Post Traumatic Stress Disorder starts acting up, the voices in my head frequently tell me to clean my shotgun as I wait for you to bring my daughter home. As soon as you pull into the drive you should exit your car with both hands in plain sight.

Speak the perimeter password, announce in a clear voice that you have brought my daughter home safely and early, then return to your car – there is no need for you to come inside. The camouflaged face at the window is mine.

MOTHERS

(THESE ONE-LINERS WOULD WORK EITHER IF YOU ARE THE MOTHER OF THE BRIDE OR GROOM, OR IF THE BRIDE IS YOUR MOTHER. TAKE YOUR PICK FROM YOUR FAVOURITES BELOW! I'VE DONE A SAMPLE LEAD-IN FOR BOTH VERSIONS.)

(IF YOU ARE THE MOTHER) *I always worked hard to try to share my own hard-earned wisdom with [name] and gave him/her specific advice. Well, on things like:*

(IF THE BRIDE IS YOUR MOTHER) *Mum always gave me such valuable advice on a whole range of important issues. You know, like on:*

Religion – 'You better pray that will come out of the carpet.'

Time travel – 'If you don't shut up, I'm going to knock you into the middle of next week!'

Logic – 'Because I said so, that's why.'

Foresight – 'Make sure you wear clean underwear, in case you're in an accident.'

Irony – 'Keep crying and I'll give you something to cry about.'

Osmosis – 'Shut your mouth and eat your tea!'

Contortionism – 'Will you 'look' at the muck on the back of your neck!'

Stamina – 'You'll sit there 'till all those sprouts are finished.'

Meteorology – 'It looks as if a hurricane swept through your room.'

Anticipation – 'You just wait and see what I'll give you when we get home!'

Astrophysics – 'If I shouted because I saw a meteor coming toward you; would you listen *then*?'

Hypocrisy – 'If I've told you once, I've told you a million times – Don't Exaggerate!!!'

The circle of life – 'I brought you into this world, and I can take you out.'

Behaviour modification – 'Stop acting like your father!'

Envy – 'There are millions of less fortunate children in this world who don't have wonderful parents like you do!'

Ophthalmology – 'If you don't stop crossing your eyes, they are going to stay like that.'

Clairvoyance – 'Put your sweater on; don't you think I know when you're cold?'

Sick humour – 'When that lawn mower cuts off your toes, don't come running to me.'

Adulthood – 'If you don't eat your vegetables, you'll never grow up.'

Genetics – 'You're just like your father.'

Genealogy – 'Do you think you were born in a barn?'

Wisdom – 'When you get to be my age, you will understand.'

Justice – 'One day you'll have kids ... and I hope they turn out just like you!'

When my sister got married, she asked to wear my mother's wedding dress. The day she tried it on for the first time I was sitting with mother in the living room as [bride] descended the stairs. The gown was a perfect fit on her petite frame. Mother's eyes welled with tears. I put my arm around her.

'You're not losing a daughter,' I reminded her in time-honoured fashion. 'You're gaining a son.'

'Oh, forget about that!' she said with a sob. 'I used to fit into that dress!'

(HOW TO PERSONALISE THIS ONE)

(IF YOU'RE THE BRIDE'S MOTHER) *When we were preparing for the wedding, at one point [bride] thought she might like to wear my wedding dress. The day she tried it on for the first time I was sitting in the living room as (bride) walked down the stairs. The dress was a perfect fit* on her petite frame. I burst into tears, so [bride] put her arm around me and said, 'don't worry Mum, you're not losing a daughter, you're gaining a son.'

'Oh, forget about that!' I said, sobbing. 'I used to fit into that dress!'

(IF YOU'RE THE BRIDE) When we were preparing for the wedding, at one point I thought I might like to wear Mum's wedding dress. The day I tried it on for the first time she was sitting in the living room as I walked down the stairs. The dress was a perfect fit. Mum burst into tears, so I put her arm around her, like you do, and said, 'Don't worry Mum, you're not losing a daughter, you're gaining a son.'

'Oh, forget about that!' she said, sobbing. 'I used to fit into that dress!'

(IF YOU'RE THE BRIDE'S SISTER) When we were preparing for the wedding, at one point [bride] thought she might like to wear Mum's wedding dress. The day she tried it on for the first time we were all sitting in the living room as [bride] walked down the stairs. The dress was a perfect fit. Mum burst into tears, so [bride] put her arm around her, like you do, and said, 'don't worry Mum, you're not losing a daughter, you're gaining a son.'

'Oh, forget about that!' she said, sobbing. 'I used to fit into that dress!'

CHILDREN

(IF WEDDING HAS TAKEN PLACE IN A CHURCH WITH A CEMETERY.) Earlier on little *[name]* and I were walking through the churchyard and she saw a gravestone that said, 'here lies John Smith, a lawyer and an honest man.' She looked up at me and said '*[however she would address you]* why would they bury two men in the same grave?

(THIS IS A SIMILAR JOKE) *Earlier on I heard one of the children ask her Mum why [bride] is dressed in white. Her Mum said, 'because white is the colour of happiness, and today is the happiest day of [bride's] life'.*

The child thought about this for a moment, then said, 'So why is the groom wearing black/grey/dark blue?'

(THIS COULD BE USED IF THE BRIDE IS PREGNANT OR THE COUPLE ARE KNOWN TO WANT TO START A FAMILY SOON. TAKE OUT A PIECE OF PAPER ON WHICH YOUR CHOICE OF THE FOLLOWING ARE WRITTEN, AND READ THEM OUT.)

I know [bride and groom] love children and plan to have several, but I think I should share a few words of warning about the whole thing. I found this series of tests written up in a very respectable parenting magazine and I just wonder if [bride and groom] would pass them all? Anyway I'd like to read out a few of them now to see what everyone thinks.

Mess test. Smear Marmite on the sofa and curtains. Now rub your hands in the wet flowerbed and rub on the walls. Cover the stains with crayons. Place a fish finger behind the settee and leave it there all summer.

Toy test. Obtain a giant box of Lego or K'nex. If those aren't available, you may substitute drawing pins or broken bottles. Have a friend spread them all over the house. Put on a blindfold. Try to walk to the bathroom or kitchen. Do not scream because this could wake a child at night.

Supermarket test. Borrow one or two small animals – goats are good – and take them with you as you shop at Tesco or Sainsburys. Always keep them in sight and pay for anything they eat or damage.

Getting Dressed test. Obtain one large, unhappy, live octopus. Stuff into a small net bag making sure that all arms stay inside.

Feeding test. Obtain a large plastic jug. Fill halfway with water. Suspend from the ceiling with a stout cord. Start the jug swinging. Try to insert spoonfuls of soggy Cocoa Pops or Cheerios into the mouth of the jug, while pretending to be an aeroplane. Now dump the contents of the jug on the floor.

Night test. Prepare by obtaining a small cloth bag and fill it with 8–12 pounds of sand. Soak it thoroughly in water. At 8:00 pm begin to waltz and hum with the bag until 9:00 pm. Lay down your bag and set your alarm for 10:00 pm. Get up, pick up your bag, and sing every song you have ever heard. Make up about a dozen more and sing these too until 4:00 am. Set alarm for 5:00 am. Get up and make breakfast. Keep this up for five years. Look cheerful.

Physical test for women. Obtain a large beanbag chair and attach it to the front of your clothes. Leave it there for nine months. Now remove 10 of the beans.

Physical test for men. Go to the nearest Boots the Chemists. Set your wallet on the counter. Ask the assistant to help himself. Now proceed to the nearest food store. Go to the head office and arrange for your entire salary to be transferred directly to the store's bank account. Purchase a newspaper. Go home and read it quietly for the last time.

Final assignment. Find a couple who already has a small child. Lecture them on how they can improve their discipline, patience, tolerance, toilet training, and child's table manners. Suggest many ways they can improve. Emphasise to them that they should never allow their children to run riot. Enjoy this experience. It will be the last time you will have all the answers.

(ALTERNATIVELY, THIS COULD BE USED IF THE BRIDE IS PREGNANT OR THE COUPLE ARE KNOWN TO WANT TO START A FAMILY SOON. TAKE OUT A PIECE OF PAPER ON WHICH YOUR CHOICE OF THE FOLLOWING ARE WRITTEN, AND READ THEM OUT.)

I know [bride and groom] love children and plan to have several, but I think I should share a few words of warning about the whole thing. I found these questions and answers in a very respectable parenting magazine and I just wonder how [bride and groom] will feel about them all. Anyway I'd like to read out a few of them now to see what everyone thinks.

Q: Should I have a baby after 35?
A: No, 35 children is enough.

Q: I'm two months pregnant now. When will my baby move?
A: With any luck, right after he finishes university.

Q: How will I know if my vomiting is morning sickness or flu?
A: If it's flu, you'll get better.

Q: What is the most common pregnancy craving?
A: For men to be the ones who get pregnant.

Q: What is the most reliable method to determine a baby's sex?
A: Childbirth.

Q: The more pregnant I get, the more often strangers smile at me. Why?
A: 'Cause you're fatter than they are.

Q: What's the difference between a nine-month pregnant woman and a supermodel?
A: Nothing – if the pregnant woman's husband knows what's good for him.

Q: My ante-natal instructor says it's not pain I'll feel during labour, but pressure. Is she right?
A: Yes, in the same way that a hurricane might be called an air current.

Q: When is the best time to get an epidural?
A: Right after you find out you're pregnant.

Q: Is there any reason why I have to be in the delivery room while my wife is in labour?
A: Not unless the word 'alimony' means anything to you.

Q: Is there anything I should avoid while recovering from childbirth?
A: Yes, pregnancy.

Q: Does pregnancy cause haemorrhoids?
A: Pregnancy causes anything you want to blame it for.

Q: What does it mean when a baby is born with teeth?
A: It means that the baby's mother may want to rethink her plans to breastfeed.

Q: What is the best time to wean the baby from breastfeeding?
A: When you see teeth marks.

(THIS ONE IS APPROPRIATE FOR A MARRIAGE WHERE THERE ARE TEENAGE CHILDREN ON ONE OR BOTH SIDES.) *I'm especially pleased to see how terrific [teenagers' names] look today, we're all incredibly proud of you. However I do know that teenagers aren't always as angelic as [names] are, and for [spouse who doesn't have teenage kids, if appropriate]'s benefit if nothing else, I'd like to share these few short comparisons between teenagers and cats.*

Neither teenagers nor cats turn their heads when you call them by name.

No matter what you do for them, it is not enough. Indeed, all human efforts are barely adequate to compensate for the privilege of waiting on them hand and foot.

You rarely see a cat walking outside of the house with an adult human being, and it can be safely said that no teenager in his or her right mind wants to be seen in public with his or her parents.

Even if you tell jokes as well as Jay Leno, neither your cat nor your teen will ever crack a smile.

No cat or teenager shares your taste in music.

Cats and teenagers can lie on the living-room sofa for hours on end without moving, barely breathing.

Cats have nine lives. Teenagers carry on as if they did.

Cats and teenagers yawn in exactly the same manner, communicating that ultimate human ecstasy – a sense of complete and utter boredom.

Cats and teenagers do not improve anyone's furniture.

Cats that are free to roam outside sometimes have been known to return in the middle of the night to deposit a dead animal in your bedroom. Teenagers are not above that sort of behaviour.

Thus, if you must raise teenagers, the best sources of advice are not other parents, but veterinary surgeons. It is also a good idea to keep a guidebook on cats at hand at all times.

And remember, above all else, put out the food and do not make any sudden moves in their direction. When they make up their minds, they will finally come to you for some affection and comfort, and it will be a triumphant moment for all concerned.

———————————

Poems – Some Samples

As with the quotations you'll find in the next chapter, these poems are my own personal favourites, and those which I would choose to read if I were giving a wedding speech. In the final chapter you'll find a number of references which will lead you to further poetry selections, so if you don't share my taste here, don't worry!

With 'classic' poems written a century or more ago there should be no problems about copyright, as beyond a given number of years after the poet's death I believe such works pass into the 'public domain' and are no longer subject to royalties when performed in a public place. Of course you could argue that a wedding is a private occasion and certainly no sensible legal system would pursue you for reading out a contemporary poem at your daughter's, sister's, or whoever's wedding.

However, if you are in any doubt whatsoever about whether or not reading a poem could constitute an infringement of copyright, please consult your legal advisers. If you don't have a legal adviser, I've included the name of a law firm I know in the Resources section of this book. If you live in the UK please consult them (or your own legal adviser) rather than take a chance. If you live in another country, please check on its copyright laws.

Please note that all the poems I have included in this chapter are in the public domain in the UK and so you can quote from them freely.

TIPS FOR READING/RECITING POETRY

Although you can memorise a poem if you want to and you're good at committing things to memory, I think it's perfectly acceptable to have it written on a piece of paper in front of you. The best option is not necessarily to memorise the whole poem, but to familiarise yourself with it sufficiently so you can just glance down occasionally to remind yourself of the words. That looks far better to the audience than if you're reading every single syllable of it.

Make sure you understand the poem so that you emphasise the right words – although you can place emphasis on the words you feel are most important for the occasion, whether the poet intended you to or not. Speak slowly and clearly. Look up frequently from the piece of paper and maintain eye contact with your audience.

MY SELECTION OF POEMS

To My Sister – William Wordsworth

IT is the first mild day of March:
Each minute sweeter than before
The redbreast sings from the tall larch
That stands beside our door.

There is a blessing in the air,
Which seems a sense of joy to yield
To the bare trees, and mountains bare,
And grass in the green field.

My sister! ('tis a wish of mine)
Now that our morning meal is done,
Make haste, your morning task resign;
Come forth and feel the sun.

Edward will come with you; –and, pray,
Put on with speed your woodland dress;
And bring no book: for this one day
We'll give to idleness.

No joyless forms shall regulate
Our living calendar:
We from to-day, my Friend, will date
The opening of the year.

Love, now a universal birth,
From heart to heart is stealing,
From earth to man, from man to earth:
–It is the hour of feeling.

One moment now may give us more
Than years of toiling reason:
Our minds shall drink at every pore
The spirit of the season.

Some silent laws our hearts will make,
Which they shall long obey:
We for the year to come may take
Our temper from to-day.

And from the blessed power that rolls
About, below, above,
We'll frame the measure of our souls:
They shall be tuned to love.

Then come, my Sister! come, I pray,
With speed put on your woodland dress;
And bring no book: for this one day
We'll give to idleness.

It Is A Beauteous Evening, Calm And Free – William Wordsworth

It is a beauteous evening, calm and free,
The holy time is quiet as a Nun
Breathless with adoration; the broad sun
Is sinking down in its tranquillity;
The gentleness of heaven broods o'er the Sea:
Listen! the mighty Being is awake,
And doth with his eternal motion make
A sound like thunder–everlastingly.
Dear Child! dear Girl! that walkest with me here,
If thou appear untouched by solemn thought,
Thy nature is not therefore less divine:

Thou liest in Abraham's bosom all the year;
And worship'st at the Temple's inner shrine,
God being with thee when we know it not.

O Nightingale! Thou Surely Art! – William Wordsworth

O nightingale! thou surely art
A creature of a 'fiery heart':–
These notes of thine–they pierce and pierce;
Tumultuous harmony and fierce!
Thou sing'st as if the God of wine
Had helped thee to a Valentine;
A song in mockery and despite
Of shades, and dews, and silent night;
And steady bliss, and all the loves
Now sleeping in these peaceful groves.
I heard a Stock-dove sing or say
His homely tale, this very day;
His voice was buried among trees,
Yet to be come at by the breeze:
He did not cease; but cooed–and cooed;
And somewhat pensively he wooed:
He sang of love, with quiet blending,
Slow to begin, and never ending;
Of serious faith, and inward glee;
That was the song–the song for me!

Addressed To My Daughter – William Wordsworth

Let us quit the leafy arbour,
And the torrent murmuring by;
For the sun is in his harbour,

Weary of the open sky.

Evening now unbinds the fetters
Fashioned by the glowing light;
All that breathe are thankful debtors
To the harbinger of night.

Yet by some grave thoughts attended
Eve renews her calm career:
For the day that now is ended,
Is the longest of the year.

Dora! sport, as now thou sportest,
On this platform, light and free;
Take thy bliss, while longest, shortest,
Are indifferent to thee!

Who would check the happy feeling
That inspires the linnet's song?
Who would stop the swallow, wheeling
On her pinions swift and strong?

Yet at this impressive season,
Words which tenderness can speak
From the truths of homely reason,
Might exalt the loveliest cheek;

And, while shades to shades succeeding
Steal the landscape from the sight,
I would urge this moral pleading,
Last forerunner of 'Good night!'

Summer ebbs; –each day that follows
Is a reflux from on high,
Tending to the darksome hollows
Where the frosts of winter lie.

He who governs the creation,
In his providence, assigned
Such a gradual declination
To the life of human kind.

Yet we mark it not; –fruits redden,
Fresh flowers blow, as flowers have blown,
And the heart is loth to deaden
Hopes that she so long hath known.

Be thou wiser, youthful Maiden!
And when thy decline shall come,
Let not flowers, or boughs fruit-laden,
Hide the knowledge of thy doom.

Now, even now, ere wrapped in slumber,
Fix thine eyes upon the sea
That absorbs time, space, and number;
Look thou to Eternity!

Follow thou the flowing river
On whose breast are thither borne
All deceived, and each deceiver,
Through the gates of night and morn;

Through the year's successive portals;
Through the bounds which many a star
Marks, not mindless of frail mortals
When his light returns from far.

Thus when thou with Time hast travelled
Toward the mighty gulf of things,
And the mazy stream unravelled
With thy best imaginings;

Think, if thou on beauty leanest,
Think how pitiful that stay,
Did not virtue give the meanest
Charms superior to decay.

Duty, like a strict preceptor,
Sometimes frowns, or seems to frown;
Choose her thistle for thy sceptre,
While youth's roses are thy crown.

Grasp it, –if thou shrink and tremble,
Fairest damsel of the green,
Thou wilt lack the only symbol
That proclaims a genuine queen;

And ensures those palms of honour
Which selected spirits wear,
Bending low before the Donor,
Lord of heaven's unchanging year!

Sonnets From The Portuguese – Elizabeth Barrett Browning

Yet, love, mere love, is beautiful indeed
And worth of acceptation. Fire is bright,
Let temple burn, or flax; an equal light
Leaps in the flame from cedar-plank or weed:
And love is fire. And when I say at need
I love thee ... mark! ... I love thee–in thy sight
I stand transfigured, glorified aright,
With conscience of the new rays that proceed
Out of my face toward thine. There's nothing low
In love, when love the lowest: meanest creatures
Who love God, God accepts while loving so.

And what I feel, across the inferior features
Of what I am, doth flash itself, and show
How that great work of Love enhances Nature's.

Sonnets From The Portuguese – Elizabeth Barrett Browning

Indeed this very love which is my boast,
And which, when rising up from breast to brow,
Doth crown me with a ruby large enow
To draw men's eyes and prove the inner cost, –
This love even, all my worth, to the uttermost,
I should not love withal, unless that thou
Hadst set me an example, shown me how,
When first thine earnest eyes with mine were crossed,
And love called love. And thus, I cannot speak
Of love even, as a good thing of my own:
Thy soul hath snatched up mine all faint and weak,
And placed it by thee on a golden throne, –
And that I love (O soul, we must be meek!)
Is by thee only, whom I love alone.

Sonnets From The Portuguese – Elizabeth Barrett Browning

If thou must love me, let it be for nought
Except for love's sake only. Do not say
'I love her for her smile–her look–her way
Of speaking gently, –for a trick of thought
That falls in well with mine, and certes brought
A sense of pleasant ease on such a day' –
For these things in themselves, Beloved, may
Be changed, or change for thee, –and love, so wrought,
May be unwrought so. Neither love me for

Thine own dear pity's wiping my cheeks dry, –
A creature might forget to weep, who bore
Thy comfort long, and lose thy love thereby!
But love me for love's sake, that evermore
Thou may'st love on, through love's eternity.

Sonnets From The Portuguese – Elizabeth Barrett Browning

How do I love thee? Let me count the ways.
I love thee to the depth and breadth and height
My soul can reach, when feeling out of sight
For the ends of Being and ideal Grace.
I love thee to the level of everyday's
Most quiet need, by sun and candlelight.
I love thee freely, as men strive for Right;
I love thee purely, as they turn from Praise.
I love thee with the passion put to use
In my old griefs, and with my childhood's faith.
I love thee with a love I seemed to lose
With my lost saints, –I love thee with the breath,
Smiles, tears, of all my life! –and, if God choose,
I shall but love thee better after death.

Proof – Emily Dickinson

That I did always love,
I bring thee proof:
That till I loved
I did not love enough.
That I shall love alway,
I offer thee
That love is life,

And life hath immortality.
This, dost thou doubt, sweet?
Then have I
Nothing to show
But Calvary.

To a Friend – Amy Lowell

I ask but one thing of you, only one,
That always you will be my dream of you;
That never shall I wake to find untrue
All this I have believed and rested on,
Forever vanished, like a vision gone
Out into the night. Alas, how few
There are who strike in us a chord we knew
Existed, but so seldom heard its tone
We tremble at the half-forgotten sound.
The world is full of rude awakenings
And heaven-born castles shattered to the ground,
Yet still our human longing vainly clings
To a belief in beauty through all wrongs.
O stay your hand, and leave my heart its songs!

Happiness – Amy Lowell

Happiness, to some, elation;
Is, to others, mere stagnation.
Days of passive somnolence,
At its wildest, indolence.
Hours of empty quietness,
No delight, and no distress.
Happiness to me is wine,

Effervescent, superfine.
Full of tang and fiery pleasure,
Far too hot to leave me leisure
For a single thought beyond it.
Drunk! Forgetful! This the bond: it
Means to give one's soul to gain
Life's quintessence. Even pain
Pricks to livelier living, then
Wakes the nerves to laugh again,
Rapture's self is three parts sorrow.
Although we must die to-morrow,
Losing every thought but this;
Torn, triumphant, drowned in bliss.
Happiness: We rarely feel it.
I would buy it, beg it, steal it,
Pay in coins of dripping blood
For this one transcendent good.

Love Me – Sara Teasdale

Brown-thrush singing all day long
In the leaves above me,
Take my love this little song,
'Love me, love me, love me!'

When he harkens what you say,
Bid him, lest he miss me,
Leave his work or leave his play,
And kiss me, kiss me, kiss me!

I Would Live In Your Love – Sara Teasdale

I would live in your love as the sea-grasses live in the sea,
Borne up by each wave as it passes, drawn down by each wave that
recedes;
I would empty my soul of the dreams that have gathered in me,
I would beat with your heart as it beats, I would follow your soul as
it leads.

To My Dear and Loving Husband – Anne Bradstreet

If ever two were one, then surely we.
If ever man were lov'd by wife, then thee;
If ever wife was happy in a man,
Compare with me ye women if you can.
I prize thy love more then whole Mines of gold,
Or all the riches that the East doth hold.
My love is such that Rivers cannot quench,
Nor ought but love from thee, give recompence.
Thy love is such I can no way repay,
The heavens reward thee manifold I pray.
Then while we live, in love let's so persever,
That when we live no more, we may live ever.

A Red, Red Rose – Robert Burns

O my luve's like a red, red rose.
That's newly sprung in June;
O my luve's like a melodie
That's sweetly play'd in tune.

As fair art thou, my bonnie lass,
So deep in luve am I;
And I will love thee still, my Dear,
Till a'the seas gang dry.

Till a' the seas gang dry, my Dear,
And the rocks melt wi' the sun:
I will luve thee still, my Dear,
While the sands o'life shall run.

And fare thee weel my only Luve!
And fare thee weel a while!
And I will come again, my Luve,
Tho' it were ten thousand mile!

Sonnet 18 – William Shakespeare

Shall I compare thee to a summer's day?
Thou art more lovely and more temperate:
Rough winds do shake the darling buds of May,
And summer's lease hath all too short a date:
Sometime too hot the eye of heaven shines,
And often is his gold complexion dimm'd;
And every fair from fair sometime declines,
By chance, or nature's changing course untrimm'd;
But thy eternal summer shall not fade,
Nor lose possession of that fair thou ow'st;
Nor shall Death brag thou wander'st in his shade,
When in eternal lines to time thou grow'st:
So long as man can breath, or eyes can see,
So long lives this, and this gives life to thee.

Sonnet 116 – William Shakespeare

Let me not to the marriage of true minds
admit impediments. Love is not love
which alters when it alteration finds,

or bends with the remover to remove:
Oh, no! It is an ever-fixed mark.
That looks on tempests and is never shaken;
it is the star to every wandering bark,
whose worth's unknown, although his height be taken.
Love's not Time's fool, though rosy lips and cheeks
within his bending sickle's compass come;
love alters not with his brief hours and weeks,
but bears it out even to the edge of doom.
If this be error and upon me proved,
I never writ, nor no man ever loved.

I Ching

When two people are at one
in their inmost hearts,
they shatter even the strength of iron or bronze.
And when two people understand each other
in their inmost hearts,
their words are sweet and strong,
like the fragrance of orchids.

Fidelity – D H Lawrence

Man and woman are like the earth, that brings forth flowers
in summer, and love, but underneath is rock.
Older than flowers, older than ferns, older than foraminiferae,
older than plasm altogether is the soul underneath.
And when, throughout all the wild chaos of love
slowly a gem forms, in the ancient, once-more-molten rocks
of two human hearts, two ancient rocks,
a man's heart and a woman's,

that is the crystal of peace, the slow hard jewel of trust,
the sapphire of fidelity.
The gem of mutual peace emerging from the wild chaos of love.

Corinthians 13:4-8 – The Bible

Love is patient and kind; love is not jealous or boastful; it is not
arrogant or rude. Love does not insist on its own way; it is not
irritable or resentful; it does not rejoice at wrong, but rejoices in
the right. Love bears all things, believes all things, hopes all
things, endures all things. Love never ends.

Marriage – Mary Weston Fordham

The die is cast, come weal, come woe,
Two lives are joined together,
For better or for worse, the link
Which naught but death can sever.
The die is cast, come grief, come joy.
Come richer, or come poorer,
If love but binds the mystic tie,
Blest is the bridal hour.

My True Love Hath My Heart – Sir Philip Sidney

My true-love hath my heart, and I have his,
By just exchange one for another given:
I hold his dear, and mine he cannot miss,
There never was a better bargain driven:

My true-love hath my heart, and I have his,
My heart in me keeps him and me in one,
My heart in him his thoughts and senses guide:

He loves my heart, for once it was his own,
I cherish his because in me it bides:

My true-love hath my heart, and I have his.

To Be One With Each Other – George Eliot

What greater thing is there for two human souls
than to feel that they are joined together to strengthen
each other in all labor, to minister to each other in all sorrow,
to share with each other in all gladness,
to be one with each other in the
silent unspoken memories?

Two Lovers – George Eliot

Two lovers by a moss-grown spring:
They leaned soft cheeks together there,
Mingled the dark and sunny hair,
And heard the wooing thrushes sing.
O budding time!
O love's blest prime!

Two wedded from the portal stept:
The bells made happy carolings,
The air was soft as fanning wings,
White petals on the pathway slept.
O pure-eyed bride!
O tender pride!

Two faces o'er a cradle bent:
Two hands above the head were locked:
These pressed each other while they rocked,

Those watched a life that love had sent.
O solemn hour!
O hidden power!

Two parents by the evening fire:
The red light fell about their knees
On heads that rose by slow degrees
Like buds upon the lily spire.
O patient life!
O tender strife!

The two still sat together there,
The red light shone about their knees;
But all the heads by slow degrees
Had gone and left that lonely pair.
O voyage fast!
O vanished past!

The red light shone upon the floor
And made the space between them wide;
They drew their chairs up side by side,
Their pale cheeks joined, and said, 'Once more!'
O memories!
O past that is!

Hindu Marriage Poem – Author unknown

You have become mine forever.
Yes, we have become partners.
I have become yours.
Hereafter, I cannot live without you.
Do not live without me.
Let us share the joys.

We are word and meaning, unite.
You are thought and I am sound.
May the nights be honey-sweet for us.
May the mornings be honey-sweet for us.
May the plants be honey-sweet for us.
May the earth be honey-sweet for us.

From This Day Forward – Author unknown

From this day forward,
You shall not walk alone.
My heart will be your shelter,
And my arms will be your home.

This Day I Married My Best Friend – Author unknown

This day I married my best friend
... the one I laugh with as we share life's wondrous zest,
as we find new enjoyments and experience all that's best.
... the one I live for because the world seems brighter
as our happy times are better and our burdens feel much lighter.
... the one I love with every fibre of my soul.
We used to feel vaguely incomplete, now together we are whole.

Apache Blessing – Author unknown

May the sun bring you new energy by day,
May the moon softly restore you by night,
May the rain wash away your worries
And the breeze blow new strength into your being,
And all the days of your life may you walk
Gently through the world and know its beauty.

Eskimo Love Song – Author unknown

You are my husband
My feet shall run because of you
My feet shall dance because of you
My heart shall beat because of you
My eyes see because of you
My mind thinks because of you
And I shall love because of you.

Quotations – Some Useful Ideas

Many people who advise speakers at weddings – and other social and business occasions, for that matter – advocate that you should use quotations gently and subtly. I agree. Overuse of quotations has a strange way of sounding rather pompous and pseudo-intellectual, which I imagine is something you don't want to emulate!

In this chapter I've gathered together some quotes which I personally like and, if I were to be giving a speech at a wedding, might well be inclined to use. Naturally there are thousands to choose from and I have indicated where you can find more in the Resources section. But hey, start your selection process with these – I think they're fab.

FAMILY

'Most of us become parents long before we have stopped being children.' – Mignon McLaughlin

'Family isn't about whose blood you have. It's about who you care about.' – Trey Parker and Matt Stone (*South Park*)

'Call it a clan, call it a network, call it a tribe, call it a family. Whatever you call it, whoever you are, you need one.' – Jane Howard

'They say that blood is thicker than water. Maybe that's why we battle our own with more energy and gusto than we would ever expend on strangers.' – David Assael

'If you cannot get rid of the family skeleton, you may as well make it dance.' – George Bernard Shaw

'Happiness is having a large, loving, caring, close-knit family in another city.' – George Burns

'Parents are the bones on which children sharpen their teeth.' – Peter Ustinov

'If you can give your son or daughter only one gift, let it be enthusiasm.' – Bruce Barton

'The best way to keep children home is to make the home atmosphere pleasant – and let the air out of the tyres.' – Dorothy Parker

'I have found the best way to give advice to your children is to find out what they want and then advise them to do it.' – Harry S Truman

'Children begin by loving their parents; as they grow older they judge them; sometimes they forgive them.' – Oscar Wilde

'Children are the only form of immortality that we can be sure of.' – Peter Ustinov

'Always be nice to your children because they are the ones who will choose your rest (retirement) home.' – Phyllis Diller

'The reason grandparents and grandchildren get along so well is that they have a common enemy.' – Sam Levenson

HAPPINESS AND LOVE

'Many persons have a wrong idea of what constitutes true happiness. It is not attained through self-gratification but through fidelity to a worthy purpose.' – Helen Keller

'The best and most beautiful things in the world cannot be seen or even touched. They must be felt within the heart.' – Helen Keller

'Too much of a good thing is wonderful.' – Mae West

'Perhaps the feelings that we experience when we are in love represent a normal state. Being in love shows a person who he should be.' – Anton Chekhov

'The meeting of two personalities is like the contact of two chemical substances: if there is any reaction, both are transformed.' – Carl Jung

'Love is everything it's cracked up to be... It really is worth fighting for, being brave for, risking everything for.' – Erica Jong

'To love is to receive a glimpse of heaven.' – Karen Sunde

'Love is not blind – it sees more, not less. But because it sees more, it is willing to see less.' – Rabbi Julius Gordon

'Before I met my husband, I'd never fallen in love, though I'd stepped in it a few times.' – Rita Rudner

'One word frees us of all the weight and pain of life: That word is love.' – Sophocles

'Cherish all your happy moments: they make a fine cushion for old age.' – Christopher Morley

'I am a kind of paranoiac in reverse. I suspect people of plotting to make me happy.' – J D Salinger

'We are all born for love. It is the principle of existence, and its only end.' – Benjamin Disraeli

'Where there is love there is life.' – Mahatma Gandhi

'The supreme happiness in life is the conviction that we are loved.'
– Victor Hugo

'Love is not the dying moan of a distant violin – it's the triumphant twang of a bedspring.' – S J Perelman

'We've got this gift of love, but love is like a precious plant. You can't just accept it and leave it in the cupboard or just think it's going to get on by itself. You've got to keep watering it, really look after it and nurture it.' – John Lennon

'There is only one happiness in life, to love and be loved.'
– George Sand

MARRIAGE

'I pay very little regard ... to what any young person says on the subject of marriage. If they profess a disinclination for it, I only set it down that they have not yet seen the right person.' – Jane Austen, *Mansfield Park*

'A great marriage is not when the 'perfect couple' comes together. It is when an imperfect couple learns to enjoy their differences.'
– Dave Meurer

'A successful marriage requires falling in love many times, always with the same person.' – Mignon McLaughlin

'All married couples should learn the art of battle as they should learn the art of making love. Good battle is objective and honest– never vicious or cruel. Good battle is healthy and constructive,

and brings to a marriage the principle of equal partnership.'
– Ann Landers

'In marriage, being the right person is as important as finding the right person.' – Wilbert Donald Gough

'To keep the fire burning brightly, there's one easy rule: keep the two logs together, near enough to keep each other warm and far enough apart – about a finger's breadth – for breathing room. Good fire, good marriage, same rule.' – Marnie Reed Crowell

'Marriage is popular because it combines the maximum of temptation with the maximum of opportunity.' – George Bernard Shaw

'Keep your eyes wide open before marriage, half-shut afterwards.'
– Benjamin Franklin

'There is no more lovely, friendly and charming relationship, communion or company than a good marriage.' – Martin Luther

'The goal in marriage is not to think alike, but to think together.'
– Robert C Dodds

'Chains do not hold a marriage together. It is threads, hundreds of tiny threads, which sew people together over the years.'
– Simone Signoret

'Marriage resembles a pair of shears, so joined that they cannot be separated; often moving in opposite directions, yet always punishing anyone who comes between them.' – Sydney Smith

'A happy marriage is a long conversation which always seems too short.' – André Maurois

'Actually a marriage in which no quarrelling at all takes place may well be one that is dead or dying from emotional undernourishment. If you care, you probably fight.' – Flora Davis

'A successful marriage is an edifice that must be rebuilt every day.' – André Maurois

'A great marriage is not when the "perfect couple" comes together.' – Dave Meurer

'Marriage. It's like a cultural hand-rail. It links folks to the past and guides them to the future.' – Diane Frolov and Andrew Schneider

'That is what marriage really means: helping one another to reach the full status of being persons, responsible and autonomous beings who do not run away from life.' – Paul Tournier

'I love being married. It's so great to find that one special person you want to annoy for the rest of your life.' – Rita Rudner

'The value of marriage is not that adults produce children but that children produce adults.' – Peter De Vries

MEN/FATHERS
'I usually make up my mind about a man in ten seconds; and I very rarely change it.' – Margaret Thatcher

'It is a wise father that knows his own child.' – William Shakespeare, *The Merchant of Venice*

'If I chance to talk a little wild, forgive me; I had it from my father.' – King Henry VIII

'Only choose in marriage a woman whom you would choose as a friend if she were a man.' – Joseph Joubert

'My parents want me to get married. They don't care who any more, as long as he doesn't have a pierced ear, that's all they care about. I think men who have a pierced ear are better prepared for marriage. They've experienced pain and bought jewellery.' – Rita Rudner

'The place of the father in the modern suburban family is a very small one, particularly if he plays golf.' – Bertrand Russell

WOMEN/MOTHERS
'The enthusiasm of a woman's love is even beyond the biographer's.' – Jane Austen

'... when a young lady is to be a heroine, the perverseness of forty surrounding families cannot prevent her. Something must and will happen to throw a hero in her way.' – Jane Austen

'A woman is like a tea bag – you never know how strong she is until she gets in hot water.' – Eleanor Roosevelt

'I am extraordinarily patient, provided I get my own way in the end.' – Margaret Thatcher

'Sooner or later we all quote our mothers.' – Bern Williams

'A mother is not a person to lean on but a person to make leaning unnecessary.' – Dorothy C Fisher

'My mother had a great deal of trouble with me, but I think she enjoyed it.' – Mark Twain

'God could not be everywhere and therefore he made mothers.' – Anon

'Heaven is at the feet of Mothers.' – Arab proverb

'For a mother is the only person on earth who can divide her love among ten children. And each child still have all her love.' – Anon

WEDDING FOLKLORE

From the Philippines (with some ideas for comments you could make)

Giving an 'arinola' (chamberpot) as a wedding gift is believed to bring good luck to newlyweds.

Aha, that means they'll really like the present I got them!

The groom who sits down before his bride does during the wedding ceremony will be a henpecked husband.

(Groom), did you sit down at all?

If it rains during the wedding, it means prosperity and happiness for the newlyweds.

Well, if that's the case this country should be full of deliriously happy married millionaires.

Throwing rice confetti at the newlyweds will bring them prosperity all their life.

Other cultures believe that throwing rice means fertility for the newlyweds, so if this one is true as well they'll need to be prosperous to pay for all those kids.

The groom must arrive at the church before the bride to avoid bad luck.

I'll tell you something if [groom] had arrived after [bride] today he'd have had more than bad luck. He'd have got both his legs broken.

Breaking something during the reception brings good luck to the newlyweds.

But that does not *mean anyone can start throwing plates or glasses!*

The bride should step on the groom's foot while walking towards the altar if she wants him to agree with her every whim.
So that's *why we had to get (bride's) Jimmy Choo stilettos reinforced with titanium!*

An unmarried woman who follows the footsteps (literally) of the newlyweds will marry soon.
Go on then girls, start lining up to follow them around the [dance floor/to the buffet/whatever is appropriate]

The months for marriage
(Original author unknown)

January
Marry when the year is new, he'll be loving, kind and true.

February
When February birds do mate, you wed nor dread your fate.

March
If you wed when March winds blow, joy and sorrow both you'll know.

April
Marry in April if you can, joy for maiden and for man.

May
Marry in the month of May, you will romance the day.

June

Marry when June roses grow and over land and sea you'll go.

July

Those who in July do wed must labour for their daily bread.

August

Whoever wed in August be, many a change is sure to see.

September

Marry in September's shine so that your life is rich and fine.

October

If in October you do marry, love will come but riches tarry.

November

If you wed in bleak November, only joys will come, remember!

December

When December's snows fall fast, marry and your love will last.

The colour of the bride's dress
(Original author unknown)

Marry in white, you've chosen him right.
Marry in blue, your love will be true.
Marry in pearl, you'll live in a whirl.
Marry in brown, you'll live out of town.
Marry in red, you'd be better off dead.
Marry in yellow, you're in love with the fellow.

Marry in green, you love being seen.
Marry in pink, your families will link!

Women proposing

There were a number of interesting ways in which marriages were made. In the Middle Ages, in England, although women had far fewer rights than men, they could propose on 29 February – Leap Year Day – because that was not an official day on the calendar. Therefore, no laws applied, and women were free of the restrictions that governed their behaviour the rest of the year. They seized the opportunity to resolve relationships that were taking too long to lead to marriage and to push indecisive suitors into action.

More commonly, especially in rural areas, a girl would peel an apple in a single paring and throw the skin over her shoulder, hoping it would land in the shape of the initial letter of her lover's name. This practice, apple paring, was carried over to North America by the pioneers, whose young women held group apple paring ceremonies to discover whom they should wed.

Excerpted from *Be the best, Best Man and Make a Stunning Speech* (How To Books) by Phillip Khan-Panni.
www.phillipkhan-panni.com/

Resources/Bibliography

The books I have recommended below are all available on *Amazon.co.uk*. If you prefer to get them from a bookshop or your nearest public library, I have included the ISBN number of each book. (That makes them easier to find on computer systems in bookshops and libraries.)

I haven't read each book described below from cover to cover, nor have I read each and every website from the home page through to its last few words. However, I have had a good look at each entry and am more than happy to recommend that you take a second look, too.

However, never forget that old, politically incorrect saying about how 'one man's meat is another man's poison'. In reading through the reviews of some of the books listed below I have been astounded – especially in the case of humorous books – at just how opposed people's views can be. But hey, that's what makes the world go around. Wouldn't life be boring if we all felt the same way about everything?

Websites affect us in the same way. Some are right up our street; some definitely are not.

All I hope to have achieved in this section of the book is to supply you with some additional ideas and inspirations to help you give *the* most amazing wedding speech ever. (My lists of books and websites are by no means exhaustive – mainly they're just the tip of the iceberg. There are many more.)

BOOKS ON HOW TO PLAN WEDDINGS

Planning Your Wedding: A Step-by-step Guide That Will Take You Right Through to the Big Day, Judith Verity (How To Books). Paperback. ISBN 1857038746. Also available from www.howtobooks.co.uk

A Modern Girl's Guide to Getting Hitched: How to Plan, Survive and Enjoy Your Wedding, Sarah Ivens (Piatkus Books). Paperback. ISBN 0749922680.

Your Day, Your Way: The Essential Handbook for the 21st-century Bride, Michelle Roth, Sharon Naylor and Henry Roth (Prima Life). Paperback. ISBN 0761525394.

The Wedding Diaries: How to Get Married in Style Without Breaking the Bank, Laura Bloom (White Ladder Press Ltd). Paperback. ISBN 0954391489.

Your Daughter's Wedding: Tips for the Mother of the Bride, Confetti Series (Conran Octopus). Paperback. ISBN 1840913061.

WEBSITES ABOUT WEDDING PLANNING AND ORGANISATION

www.hitched.co.uk

www.weddings.co.uk

www.weddingguide.co.uk

weddings-and-brides.co.uk

www.confetti.co.uk

www.silverlinings.co.uk

weddingchaos.co.uk

paler.com/wedding_planning.html

www.net-weddings.co.uk

www.weddingplanner.co.uk

www.our-wedding-plans.co.uk

www.pinkproducts.co.uk (gay and lesbian weddings)

www.committed2pink.co.uk (gay and lesbian weddings)

www.confetti.co.uk (gay and lesbian weddings)

www.yourdreamshaadi.co.uk (Asian weddings)

www.confetti.co.uk (Hindu weddings)

www.weddingguide.co.uk (Hindu, Sikh weddings)

www.whichwedding.co.uk (Roman Catholic, Sikh, gay/lesbian and other weddings)

www.somethingjewish.co.uk/articles/951_jewish_weddings.htm (Jewish weddings)

confetti.co.uk (Jewish weddings)

www.weddingguide.co.uk (Jewish weddings)

www.confetti.co.uk (Buddhist weddings)

www.whichwedding.co.uk (Buddhist weddings)

weddingguide.co.uk (Muslim weddings)

www.confetti.co.uk (Muslim weddings)

www.whichwedding.co.uk (Muslim weddings)

OTHER BOOKS ON WEDDING SPEECHES

Make a Great Wedding Speech, Philip Calvert (How To Books).
Paperback. ISBN 184528027X. Also available from
www.howtobooks.co.uk
Philip Calvert's website: www.cirisbiz.co.uk

*Making a Wedding Speech: How to Face the Big Occasion with
Confidence and Carry It Off with Style*, John Bowden (How To
Books). Paperback. ISBN 1857036603. Also available from
www.howtobooks.co.uk

Making The Best Man's Speech, John Bowden (How To Books).
Paperback. ISBN 185703659X. Also available from
www.howtobooks.co.uk

Making the Bridegroom's Speech, John Bowden (How To Books).
Paperback. ISBN 1857035674. Also available from
www.howtobooks.co.uk

Making the Father of the Bride's Speech, John Bowden (How To Books).
Paperback. ISBN 1857035682. Also available from
www.howtobooks.co.uk

Be the best Best Man and Make a Stunning Speech, Phillip Khan-Panni
(How To Books). Paperback. ISBN 1857038029. Also available from
www.howtobooks.co.uk
Phillip Khan-Panni's website:
www.phillipkhan-panni.com/

THESAURUS RESOURCES

Roget's Thesaurus of English Words and Phrases, edited by George
Davidson, (Penguin Books). Paperback. ISBN 0140515038.
www.dictionary.reference.com (online dictionary and thesaurus)

WEBSITES OFFERING FREE HELP WITH WEDDING SPEECHES

www.hitched.co.uk (sample wedding speeches – bride, maid of honour,
best woman)
www.weddingspeechbuilder.com (bride's speech)
www.presentationhelper.co.uk/wedding_speech.htm
www.confetti.co.uk (bride's speech)
www.weddingguide.co.uk (bride's speech)

WEBSITES OFFERING PAID-FOR HELP WITH WEDDING SPEECHES

www.speechesforweddings.com
www.finespeeches.com/ (male speakers only, but probably would help
women too)
www.sparklingspeeches.co.uk
www.wedding-speech.org
www.speeches.com
www.personalisedweddingspeeches.co.uk

READY-MADE WEDDING SPEECHES YOU COULD CANNIBALISE

www.wedding-speeches.org/
www.free-wedding-speeches.com
www.ultimatespeeches.com
www.hitched.co.uk

SPEECHWRITERS IN THE UK

Hiring a speechwriter isn't cheap, but if after reading this book you still
feel you need some help here is a selection of people you can contact in
an emergency. Bear in mind, too, that I and many of my colleagues offer

an editing service whereby we will give your own writing efforts a professional polish. That usually costs much less than having the speech written from scratch.

In the nicest possible way I hope that – thanks to this book – you won't need us, but here are some names and email addresses just in case.

Suzan St Maur
Email: suze@suzanstmaur.com
Website: www.suzanstmaur.com

Philip Calvert
Email: philip@philipcalvert.com
Website:www.philipcalvert.com

Katherine Trimble
Email: katherine@gaelkat.com
Website: www.gaelkat.com

Caroline Lashley
Email: info@theeditorsoffice.co.uk
Website: www.theeditorsoffice.co.uk

BOOKS ON IMPROVING YOUR PRESENTING SKILLS

The Little Big Voice: Voice Coaching for Ordinary People, Dr Simon Raybould (Piquant). Paperback. ISBN 1903689155.
Dr Raybould's website: www.curved-vision.co.uk
Like A Brick Wrapped In Velvet, Dr Simon Raybould. eBook. Available from: www.velvetbrick.co.uk/
Dr Raybould's website: www.curved-vision.co.uk
Presenting with Power: Never Again Be Boring – Overcome Those Nerves – Deliver with Style, Shay McConnon (How To Books). Paperback. ISBN 1845280229. Also available from www.howtobooks.co.uk
The Vocal Skills Pocketbook, Richard Payne (Management Pocketbooks). Paperback. ISBN 1903776171.

LIVE VOICE AND PRESENTATION TRAINING
Telling People
with Dr Simon Raybould
www.tellingpeople.co.uk/

Philip Calvert
Executive Speech Coach and Presentation Expert
www.philipcalvert.com

BOOKS ON WRITING JOKES AND COMEDY
Comedy Writing Secrets: How to Think Funny, Write Funny, Act Funny and Get Paid for It, Mel Helitzer and Mark Schatz (Writer's Digest Books). Paperback. ISBN 1582973571.
The Comic Toolbox: How to Be Funny If You're Not, John Vorhaus (Silman-James Press). Paperback. ISBN 1879505215.

WEBSITES ABOUT HOW TO WRITE JOKES
www.users.totalise.co.uk/~tmd/jokes.htm
www.vt.essortment.com/writejokes_rcej.htm
www.humormall.com
www.comedy-zone.net

BOOKS OF JOKES
Man Walks into a Bar: The Ultimate Collection of Jokes and One-liners, Stephen Arnott and Mike Haskins (Ebury Press). Paperback. ISBN 0091897653.
Jokes, Toasts and One-Liners for Wedding Speeches: Original Lines to Make Them Laugh and Cry, Confetti Series (Conran Octopus). Paperback. ISBN 1840913703.
Friars Club Encyclopedia of Jokes: Over 2000 One-Liners, Straight Lines, Stories, Gags, Roasts, Ribs, and Put-Downs, edited by H Aaron Cohl, (Black Dog & Leventhal Publishers Inc). Paperback. ISBN 1884822630.
The Public Speaker's Joke Book, Kevin Goldstein-Jackson (Elliot Right Way Books). Paperback. ISBN 0716020718.

Mitch Murray's One Liners for Speeches for Special Occasions, Mitch
Murray (Foulsham). Paperback. ISBN 057202388X.

WEBSITES THAT PROVIDE JOKES

Be warned; there are thousands – probably hundreds of thousands – of
jokes websites on the internet and the vast majority use the same jokes
as everyone else does, most of which aren't very funny anyway. And on
top of that most internet jokes are either smutty or aimed at bright six-
year-olds. However here I've suggested a few sites that offer jokes of a
slightly more appropriate standard.

www.jokeaday.com
www.broadcaster.org.uk/section2/jokes/parentingjokes.html
www.splitsides.com

Now – if, like me, you find that internet jokes just don't do it for you,
contact me – I have a database of several thousand jokes I think are
funny and would be glad to share appropriate ones with you, so you can
personalise them for your speech. Email me at *suze@suzanstmaur.com*. If
all you want is one or two I won't charge you any money, but if it gets
to more than an hour or so of my time I will have to send you bill – if I
don't my accountant will never speak to me again.

BOOKS ON HOW TO WRITE POETRY

In the Palm of Your Hand: The Poet's Portable Workshop, Steve Kowit
(Atlantic Books). Hardcover. ISBN 0884481492.
Writing Poetry (Writing Handbooks Series), John Whitworth (A & C
Black). Paperback. ISBN 0713658223.
The Poet's Manual and Rhyming Dictionary, Frances Stillman (Thames
and Hudson Ltd). Paperback. ISBN 0500270309.
Oxford Rhyming Dictionary, edited by Clive Upton and Eben Upton,
(Oxford University Press). Hardcover. ISBN 0192801155.
Writing Poems, Peter Sansom (Bloodaxe Books). Paperback. ISBN
1852242043.

WEBSITES THAT HELP YOU WRITE YOUR OWN POETRY

resources4poets.homestead.com/
www.poetrymagic.co.uk
www.rhymezone.com
www.rhymer.com
www.bbc.co.uk/arts/poetry/wordplay/

BOOKS OF POETRY TO CHOOSE FROM

The New Penguin Book of Romantic Verse, edited by Jonathon
  Wordsworth, (Penguin Books Ltd). Paperback. ISBN 0140435689.
English Romantic Poetry: An Anthology, edited by Stanley Appelbaum
  (Dover Publications). Paperback. ISBN 0486292827.
Love Poems, edited by Sheila Kohler, Peter Washington and Kevin
  Young (Everyman's Library). Hardcover. ISBN 0679429069.
The Nation's Favourite Love Poems, Daisy Goodwin (BBC Books).
  Paperback. ISBN 056338378X.
Wedding Readings: Poetry and Prose for Church and Civil Weddings,
  Confetti Series (Conran Octopus). Paperback. ISBN 1840912294.
Poems and Readings for Weddings, Julia Watson (Penguin Books Ltd).
  Paperback. ISBN 0141014954.

WEBSITES TO HELP YOU CHOOSE POETRY

www.poemhunter.com/
www.poets.org/
www.emule.com/poetry/
www.bl.uk/collections/wider/poet.html#otherpoet
www.poetry-portal.com/
www.lovepoemsandquotes.com/
www.netpoets.com/poems/

LEGAL ADVICE REGARDING COPYRIGHT ETC

Andrew Woolley
www.business-lawfirm.co.uk

DATES THROUGHOUT HISTORY

As it happens I have a database of dates through history covering all 365 days of the year and although I can't vouch absolutely for their accuracy, I would be glad to share them with you. They would be easy enough to verify on an individual basis via the internet or other reference sources. Email me on *suze@suzanstmaur.com*. In the meantime, here are some other resources.

Books

On This Day: Over 2000 Years of Front-Page History, edited by Sian Facer (Gramercy Books). Hardcover. ISBN 0517226316.

The 'Time Team' Guide to What Happened When, Tim Taylor and Matthew Reynolds (Channel Four Books/Transworld). Hardcover. ISBN 1905026099.

Websites

www.news.bbc.co.uk/onthisday/default.stm (BBC News website)

www.thehistorychannel.co.uk/site/this_day_in_history

www.uk.dir.yahoo.com/Arts/Humanities/History/This_Day_in_History/ (a portal, listing dozens of further relevant sites including those covering various different countries and cultures)

www.allheadlinenews.com/todayinhistory/

www.gaytoz.com/bGay_Dates.asp (dates of relevance to gay/lesbian community)

BOOKS ON QUOTATIONS

The Oxford Dictionary of Quotations by Subject, edited by Susan Ratcliffe (Oxford University Press). Paperback. ISBN 0198607504.

The Oxford Dictionary of Humorous Quotations, edited by Ned Sherrin (Oxford University Press). Paperback. ISBN 0198609205.

The Funniest Thing You Never Said: The Ultimate Collection of Humorous Quotations, Rosemarie Jarski (Ebury Press). Paperback. ISBN 0091897661.

Chick Wit: Over 1000 Wisecracks from 21st Century Women, Jasmine Birtles (Prion Books Ltd). Paperback. ISBN 1853755389.

Words of Love: Romantic Quotations from Plato to Madonna, edited by
Joseph Krevisky and Jordan L. Linoleum (Random House USA
Inc). Paperback. ISBN 0679777199.

WEBSITES FOR QUOTATIONS
www.quotationspage.com/
www.quoteland.com/
www.creativequotations.com/
www.aphids.com/quotes/index.shtml
www.quotesandsayings.com/
www.saidwhat.co.uk/
www.comedy-zone.net/quotes/
www.william-shakespeare.info/william-shakespeare-quotes.htm
www.aardvarkarchie.com/quotes/marriage5.htm

WEDDING MAGAZINES
www.reviewcentre.com/products736.html (reviews of popular magazines)
www.weddings-and-brides.co.uk/features/featureaug.htm (reviews of
popular magazines)

HOW TO SEARCH ONLINE
Books
The Good Web Site Guide, Graham Edmonds (HarperCollins).
Paperback. ISBN 0007193858.
The Rough Guide to the Internet, Duncan Clark, Peter Buckley (Rough
Guides). Paperback. ISBN 1843535505.

Websites
www.google.com/help/basics.html
www.libraryspot.com/features/searchenginetips.htm

Index